# There

## A Place in God's Will

## Willie M.V. Stephens
## (VeLeJouSte)

authorHOUSE®

*AuthorHouse™*
*1663 Liberty Drive*
*Bloomington, IN 47403*
*www.authorhouse.com*
*Phone: 1-800-839-8640*

*First published by AuthorHouse 10/30/2009*

*ISBN: 978-1-4389-8394-3 (sc)*

*Printed in the United States of America*
*Bloomington, Indiana*

*This book is printed on acid-free paper.*

*You will notice that some words or sayings
in one or more chapters are repeated in another.*

*That is for memory strengthening, giving the reader
the ability to voluntarily remember (learn by heart).*

*Both parents provided incentives, for my brothers, sisters, and I.*
*They stressed adherence, to God and His Statutes.*
*They emphasized high morals, which motivated us to want to*
*do right in our talks and walks.*
*Mom being more verbal, She lectured and taught, some were*
*repetitious, still we never tired hearing them.*
*Conversely Daddy's influence was voiceless, but was portrayed*
*in His body language, which the family translated well.*
*His influential rearing pattern was powerful.*
*Both of our parents teamed in rearing us.*
*Their upbringing affected us also others in a beautiful way.*
*That which they taught us was embraced and utilized.*

*I thank The Creator for having loaned us Parents, Who Cared!*

*Willie M V Stephens*
*VeLeJouSte*

# Acknowledgements

First I dedicate this book to an awesome God, without whose love,
And wisdom, this book would not have been brought into being.

My sincere gratitude to all who were, and are behind my efforts.

My deceased parents, Paul Veazie, and Lillian Leday Veazie, My
deceased husband, Martin M. Stephens, Sr. without whose words, and
faith in me, I would have ceased to write.

Our nine children, their husbands, wives, and their families, without
Whose encouraging words, and help, this book would not exist.

With elation and love, I thank God for each pastor,
Evangelist, Missionary,
And all others who taught, and inspired me,
through sermons, lectures, and Exhortations.

My Prayers, and Gratitude to the entire Staff of AuthorHouse.

Willie M. V. Stephens,

VeLeJouSte

# There

Webster's definition of "there" reads as follows: at or in that place, etc.

The "There" that is to be read about is a created place of God, who created offspring to have fellowship with, offspring to praise and worship Him.

There – a place for those who are called by His name, professing His salvation, to abide therein. Not on the edge, but in the heart of it – with a made up mind to remain. Persistent praying through faith will move God to give one what it takes to remain. God doesn't only need our faith, but our will also.

This There cannot be prefixed with words such as "near, around, thereby, thereat," or "thereabouts." But, single, distinct from any other. One as God is one, and may be named therein, into, or in there. A sacred, non-fringed place of an awesome God, anchored on a solid foundation, which is the rock Jesus, our Lord and Savior: the beginning, and the end.

We should beseech Him to fortify us with what it takes to inhabit and remain therein, There. To remain in solidness is pleasing to our Maker and Provider – without omission of any occasion, let endurance rule with a succinct attitude. All believers need a strong foundation for their services. Many simulate words or meanings, especially when it concerns God or His word. Many are ambivalent towards God and His will, preferring to remain in obscurities, which, for them, are pleasures in exchange – not realizing that the end thereof is an open door to a burning hell.

On the other hand, some have accepted and begun serving Our Lord, but turned back. In Paul's final writing to Timothy, he wrote of those who had turned away:

*II Timothy 4:10:* *For Demas hath forsaken me, having loved this present world and is departed.*

*II Timothy 4:16:* *At my first answer, no man stood with me, but all men forsook me, I pray God that it may not be laid to their charge.*

Even being forsaken by some, still Paul had love for his forsakers, asking God to not lay it to their charge.

Over and over, Jesus talked, and talks, about love. Being There is love. Being There is being in God's will, in His plan, growing and living in it. Richly bringing honor to Him with all fruits of the spirit woven inside, with one accord, faithfully operating in God's will, each demonstrating an initiated role of God, spiritually, in the joy of the Lord's strength.

My spiritual mind's eye visualizes a special place in God. There, that God initiated place, that plateau, a special God place, devoted to a special purpose.

There, where it pleases Him for me or anyone claiming to be His obedient, trustworthy offspring, without qualms or complaints about discomfort known to plague; those having a will to be There, that God initiated place, that plateau wherein obedience to His Will is lived by His offspring in deep-seated peace.

To be There means to be completely in God's will.

If I am not There, I am not in His Will. There is a peace which comes with having a right relation with God, free from worrisome sin. I must be dead to sin, and alive to God's Will. I must know the Lord for myself; though my old man being crucified with Christ and not a believer in Him, I am still natural, fleshly. Being in this state, I am not There. Works without faith is dead.

But, if I have faith and live by the spirit, I will die, but in the death of Christ. This is the death that gets rid of pride, fleshly self-uplifting. Sins' heights produce falls. God hates pride.

My attitude must not support my flesh, giving it a high ride. If I die the death in Christ Jesus, and regress, substituting self (flesh) for spirit, I am not There.

*Depend not on our arms of flesh*

*But upon the arms of the Almighty*

*Allow Him to untangle from pride's mesh*

If, in my failure I return to Jesus in repentance, die in Him, remain in His will, allowing Him to crucify my flesh, purge me with spiritual hyssop, sweep me with the broom of bison, circumcise my heart, planting the seed of His love of deep roots, he is the head of my life as my spirit mind and crucified flesh, magnify Him, while under His domain. I must be sold out to Him. A slave for my Lord, Father Jesus, who has omnipotent power. A just master, a rightful judge – a non-respecter of person. I need to not only have a relationship with Him, I need to know Him. If I know Him, being in His Will, then I am There.

I am His offspring, an heir of His. In His name, I want to heed His command and obey; stay in His realm, in His secret tabernacle, under the shadow of His wing.

I must work in His vineyard and field of harvest, as He works through me. In Him, I am strong, even when I am weak. I must live in Him, and He in me. This is what lodges in the height of my intellect. He is my father. With His shed blood, He redeemed me, whom He had begotten. He has a saving plan: belief, repentance, baptism in His name, baptism of the Holy Ghost, the first four steps. Because of such a father, I am heir to multiple blessings. I must allow His will and word to govern me, instead of my own. When commissioned by Him, I must persevere with bold will. I beseech Him to make me brave as a lion, and humble as a dove. If I am not humble, I am not There.

In Him, There is love, peace and joy. Without such a father, all of this would be impossible. It is all in Him.

His spiritual food and living water strengthen me spiritually.

If I claim that God is my father and I His offspring, and I obeyed by getting into His plan, made a complete turn, got baptized in His name, Jesus; received His Holy Ghost with the evidence of that heavenly language (speaking in other tongues) as the Spirit gives the utterance; continue His step-by-step growth; have the knowledge that obeying His Word, going through the God-initiated steps, is not all, but only the beginning and if I should sit back on my lees, and allow myself to get smugly comfortable in the initial phase, becoming stunted, which means failure to grow – then, I defeat the purpose of going through the first steps. This is displeasing to Our Lord; therefore, I crucify Him.

I need as He wills, to grow spiritually, and in other things pleasing to Him. Seeking more for the things of Him, growing in such, with a strong growth of penetrable roots deeply in Him; with a panting thirst for Him and His statutes. And when my thirst is sufficed by the deepness of His well, then will I be made strong. I shall receive spiritual insight, which leads into paths of righteousness.

By that strength and insight, then shall I be able to survive in the dimensions of His will, bringing fruits, service, even fruits for repentance. For, there are many souls in the fields of harvest. I beseech Him to endow me with a soul-winning mentality. I must operate faithfully in the fruits of the spirit – all of them in accord. That is, all of the fruits of the spirit, woven into my spirit and will to satisfy the initiated role of God. I must be spiritually willing, working with zeal, ungrudgingly in accord with His will, knowing that He is with me as I operate in His joy, which is my strength.

I need to be fruitful in season and out of season. Meaning, constantly to be spiritually fructified, faithfully bearing or causing to bear fruits for the Kingdom.

If I do not produce fruits to add to the ones God bless me with, I am as the man in the Bible, who was given a talent, but did not make investment to produce more. There were disappointments when the Master returned.

If I operate in like manner, I am not There.

The characteristics of God should be modeled by me. Love, joy, peace, long-suffering, gentleness, goodness, faith, meekness, and temperance.

Striving always to be in His will, having a deep communication with Him, even outside of the comfort zone, strongly in the faith. Surrendering myself to His will. In and outside of the vineyard, having a burden for the lost in and outside of the house of God. Being a willing, walking epistle.

I must live this earthly life in a fashion to ignite men, women, girls and boys to come dine and sup with the Lord. That they be so illuminated; that others beholding them will be enriched with a zeal to seek first the Kingdom of God and His righteousness. Having a hunger for His plan to accept and ever embrace. Therefore, if my life does not portray God, I am not There.

I have and still travel near and far from our home base as a driver or passenger in used or new vehicles, large and small, limousines, buses of different kinds, trains, boats, humongous ships of the oceans, small ones, too.

Flights on many, many planes – local, regional, and foreign – beholding the handiworks of God. Have lodged in some of the world's richest and most beautiful places. Dined with both rich and poor; told some about God's plan. Have eaten some of the most expensive foods. Wore expensive apparel, also head and footwear, and more.

All being benefits provided by God, I count all a blessing in the bonds of His love. Most of all, I count it a privileged blessing to witness to different ones on or off rides and flights.

Still, if I do not have what is required to be in God's will, to be in His initiated plan, with His word digested and alive inside of me, no matter how much I travel, abide; or how much my eyes behold the handiwork of the Creator, though I witness to the lost – if I do not remain, keeping my eyes on Him, to be found in His There, when this earthly house (body of mine) dissolves, If I am not There, then I will not be eligible to reign with Him – and therefore, ever be.

*II Corinthians 4:18: While we look not at the things which are seen, but at the things which are not seen for the things which are seen are temporal, but the things which are not seen are eternal.*

*II Corinthians 5:1 For we know that if our earthly house of this tabernacle were dissolved, we have a building of God, a house not made with hands, eternal in the heavens.*

While in my youth, I concluded that all on this planet is vain, perishable. Only what is done in Jesus, and the word of God, shall forever be. God said heaven and earth shall pass away, but my Word shall never!

Though souls are in God's plan, because of seeds by God's grace I have planted; and if I have not the charity of God, esteeming and magnifying Him above all else, rather embracing luxurious items and things of this earth – not praising and thanking Him, knowing that He is the provider – then, I am not There.

There! That God-initiated place.

*My life must be lived to draw men, women, boys and girls*

*To repentance, and enter God's will to forever stay*

*With never a desire to return to embrace the world*

*To keep a hunger for the Lord, even when enemies say*

*Come back where pleasure palaces are decked in pearl.*

God must be recognized in me. The work He commissioned me to do by His strength must be done with an illumination that ignites the minds of others to have a will and zeal to seek first the Kingdom of God and His righteousness.

*Oh I want to be planted in that place never to depart*

*Yes that God initiated place.*

*There, of straight and narrow way*

*With the love and fear of God deep in my heart*

*So that I can operate by His will, both night and day.*

God Omnipotent has an eternal plan. His Power, Majesty and Beauty are beyond all, no other is stronger, greater, or more beautiful. Even his word is power, and swifter than any double-edged sword. The devil and/or our flesh puts evil thoughts in minds, but God provides power to prevent yielding to sinister temptation. A Power that we need to faithfully obtain and utilize. Then, self-willed introversion would be prevented. Also, God has set non-derogatory guidelines of love for His offspring to abide by. His commands are still valid, and will forever be. He forbids acts which bring sin, ruin and shame. Sin separates from God. Think before committing sin; be reminded of its consequences, hug God's instructions. Let us not lay our heads in the devil's lap, allowing him to take possession of our lives. Are we being influenced by others, or are we influencing them, to step into There? That initiated place of God's will? If we are, then we are There. We do not have to be lost to a burning hell. Therefore, we shall step into God's saving plan, and by His Grace, we shall remain There!

In the Book of Genesis, we read about how God regretted that He created humanity. Now, Noah, being a man of God, found grace in the eyes of God; therefore, he was in that There place, where one is fit to be used by the Creator, God. Because of the wickedness of His created offspring, He was grieved, expressing sorrow for what they did with a grieved heart. Our sin breaks God's heart, just as it did in Noah's time.

God told Noah that the end of all flesh is come before me. Make me an ark. Noah obeyed, following God's instructions in constructing the ark. After the ark was built, God established a covenant with Noah: he and his family would enter the ark, and be saved. Also, he ordered Noah to take pairs of every animal into the ark; also, animals for sacrifice and food to eat. And God caused it to rain upon the face of the earth. The flood was forty days upon the earth, destroying all flesh. Because of Noah's walk with God, his faith and obedience – being There! – where he needed to be in God – he and his family were saved. What a blessing to be There, away from that which takes possession of our lives in an evil way which leads to destruction and loss – and miss being There.

Obey God with zealous faith; be prepared to be There today!

Enoch did not experience death because he was definitely There. Where? In God's will, when He, Almighty God, was ready for him to exit this earth. Therefore, he was taken directly to heaven without being visited by the death angel.

**Genesis 5:24:** *And Enoch walked with God,
and he was not: for God took him.*

**Matthew 11:5:** *Enoch was translated that he should not see death; and was not found; for before his translation he had this testimony, that he pleased God.*

To please God means to be There. Where? In God's will! Today forever There is where God wants His offspring to be truly. Enoch was There.

Joseph was There, where he needed to be in God, when he told Potifar's wife, "I would be sinning against God," when she tried so hard to seduce him. He ran from her. When evil presents temptation, we do well to flee, rather than remain to be taken by a spirit of yielding to sin, transgressing God's Law. I see Joseph as being a type of Christ. His faith was rooted and grounded in his Creator; also, he was obedient, with a diligent and positive attitude. He was sold, made a slave, imprisoned, falsely accused; still, faithfully, he remained There, where God willed him to be. Being There, God turned all this evil around. When the king recognized that the Spirit of God was in Joseph; he was moved quickly to the top. Yes, from walled-in prison to the King's palace. Having favor with God, being There, where one is eligible to be chosen king. It is rewarding to endure in God's Kingdom, to be There.

According to God's Omniscient Knowledge, time was right that He should commission Moses to go to Egypt Land, to bring the children of Israel by His power out of the Land of Egypt, where they were being afflicted. Moses had some inadequacies for such a tough mission, which he complained to God about; but He is Great, surpassing human knowledge. He offered resources to help Moses. Along with His power, He had many. Being God Omniscient saw that Moses was the viable vessel to work through in bringing about His plan. In obedience, Moses fueled the growth of whatever little zeal he did have to undertake the assignment. He came to a place of agreement; being There, Moses pleased God. His feet were shod with the Preparation of the Gospel

Shoes, and the wisdom and knowledge to lead the children, through God's power.

People called by God are the right ones for His assigned duties. He sees in terms of not just what we are, but what we will become.

After Moses died, to replace him, a smooth transition was made. During Moses' reign, Joshua walked in His footsteps, being a great arm-bearer, in obedience, with zealous speed. Therefore, he was prepared for the tomorrow, when time presented a need for a leader. In Moses' stead, because of his obedience and faith in God, he was chosen by God because he was There, There! Where? In God's will, where he needed to be. Also, after having assisted Moses in leading the children of Israel, surely he was really There, where one is eligible to be chosen by God to lead His people. And God Omniscient knew it. He knows the right time, place and vessel (person) for each of His jobs.

And Ruth said to her mother-in-law, "Entreat me not to leave you or to return from following you. For, where you go I will go; where you lodge I will lodge; your people shall be my people, your God my God. Where you die I will die, and there will I be buried." Ruth was talking to her deceased husband's mother; though he was dead, still she persevered to be an arm-bearer to his mother. What love! It was that love and faith which produced a man of God husband for Ruth. His name was Boaz. In that union, a son was conceived and brought forth; his name was Obed. Obed came to be grandfather of King David; an awesome lineage was formed, not only physically, but spiritually, also. Because, through this lineage, Jesus came. Therefore, God's plan manifested through the Holy Ghost commingled with the love of Ruth to spearhead this awesome journey of the Creator's plan. A direct line, from yonder, here to There! Where God could miraculously use the power of the Holy Ghost to impregnate Mary, a young virgin. Through this Holy Conceivement, the word was made flesh and brought forth, our Lord and Saviour Jesus Christ!

Both Ruth and Mary were There! Where God could use them.

Hannah was one of the women of the Bible who grieved because she had not conceived. Among them, she was the most prayerful; each year, she went with her husband to the tabernacle to worship God. There, she beseeched God for a son. Being faithful, having the right frame of mind, she was not only in the right place (building), but most importantly, she was in God's initiated There, the place pleasing to God, where He hears and answers intercessory prayers of faith such as Hannah uttered.

Eli, the Priest, noticed her countenance as she prayed out of the deepness of her soul. He thought that she was drunk from strong drinks. She told him that she was as woman of sorrowful spirit, as she poured out her soul to the God of Israel.

The Priest Eli told her to go in peace, and that the God of Israel would grant her petition. Being There! Therefore, her petitions were heard and answered. God blessed her womb. She conceived; and in due time, brought forth a Blessed Man Child in Ramah. Yes, a worthy son by a worthy, faithful mother. He was named Samuel. Now, Hannah promised God that, if He would give her a son, she would dedicate the child to Him, to serve with the priest. She kept her promise. After the child was weaned, she took him to the tabernacle and left him There, where he would serve God under the priest.

Samuel is another I see as a type of Christ. He became a prophet, a priest, and a judge. Truly, he was placed in God's There, even before he was born . . . There! Where he was mightily used by The Creator of it all! God's There! Surely, victory comes on the mount of intercessory. Praise God!

Elizabeth had favor with God. Therefore, she was in a God-initiated place. Being There, she was chosen by God to conceive, bear and bring forth a special child who would be the forerunner and way-preparer for the coming Messiah Jesus, whom her cousin Mary would bring forth through the powerful Plan of God Omnipotent.

*Luke 1:57: Now Elizabeth's full time came that she would be delivered, and she brought forth a son in her old age. Her neighbors and cousins rejoiced with her. They called his name Zacharias after his father, but his mother said not so. He shall be called John."*

The name God had the angel to give them for the child. Zacharias prophesied the coming of a Savior, who would redeem His people. Their son John would prepare the way. Zacharias was filled with the Holy Ghost. Truly, both Elizabeth and Zacharias were There, where God could mightily use them.

Mary was special, having the right lifestyle; therefore, she was in favor with God. She was in His special, initiated place for young girls to be. Being There, God could use her to carry out a very special plan of His. She was the type of vessel to be impregnated by the Holy Ghost, with a son of the highest. God sent the Angel Gabriel to relay the message to Mary.

*Luke 1:26:* *The Angel Gabriel was sent from God: and the Angel said unto her Fear not Mary; for you have found favor with God; behold you shall conceive in your womb and bring forth a son, and shall call his name Jesus. The Holy Ghost shall come upon you; also, that Holy Thing which shall be born of you shall be called the Son of God.*

Now, this was a miracle announcement; but when one is There, there in God's will, awesome miracles take place – through God's will. Mary was There.

Paul begins his story as a persecutor of Jesus' followers, but he was met by Jesus on the road which led to Damascus; therefore, he was transformed. Paul became a believer in Jesus, a soul-winner rather than a murderer.

*The Acts 9:3:* *As he journeyed he came near Damascus; suddenly there shined a light round about him from heaven, and he fell to the earth. He heard a voice saying to him, Saul!*

*Saul! Why do you persecute me? And he said, Who are you,*
*Lord? The Lord said, I am Jesus, whom you persecute; it is*
*hard for you to kick against the pricks. He, trembling and*
*astonished, asked, What will you have me to do?*
*The Lord said to him, Arise; go into the city, and you*
*will be told what to do."*

God assigned Ananias to meet with him. After being with
Christians in Damascus, Paul went to the synagogue to tell
the Jews about Jesus Christ. He became totally sold out to
Jesus. He let God have all that he was. Therefore, he became
eligible to be – There, where one needs to be, in Jesus. No
one except for Jesus was a great historian of Christianity like
the Apostle Paul. But, Jesus, the Greatest and Greater than
Great, through His omnipotent power, is able to change persecutors of His word, and place them in His initiated There!
The There of His will. Even his name was changed from Saul
to Paul. A new name! Praise God!

Paul was deeply rooted There!

# Love

The character of God should be seen in me: love, patience, forgiveness, dying to self, kindness and faithfulness;

Believing in God, allowing Him to be Lord of me, I must surrender my being to His will, having that special relationship with Him. I must know Him through miracles He has performed for me and/or others; there must be a deep communication between us. I must be in love with Him.

**Deuteronomy 6:5:** *God, speaking,*
*Thou shall love the Lord thy God with all thy heart,*
*and with all thy soul, and with all thy might.*

The love that lasts with a cohesiveness. A love that fights against transgression of God's command. A love in the heart's depth.

**Deuteronomy 6:6:** *And these words which I command*
*thee this day shall be in thine heart.*

When the scribes ask Jesus, which is the first commandment of all,

> ***Mark 12:29:*** *Jesus answered,*
> *The first commandment of all the commandments:*
> *the Lord our God is one Lord.*

> ***Mark 12:30:*** *And thou shall love the Lord thy God*
> *with all thy heart and all thy soul and with all thy mind*
> *and with all thy strength – this is the first commandment.*

> ***Mark 12:31:*** *And the second is like namely this,*
> *Thou shall love thy neighbor as thyself;*
> *there is none other commandment greater than these.*

Now, these are commandments of God; if I do not obey, if I can't love as God commanded, I am not There. If I am not, surely I need to entreat the Lord to instill that agape love into the depth of me to forever rein and share. I need to beseech Him to help me get – There! There, where it is God's will. True obedience comes from the heart, with love. I am to demonstrate that love.

> ***Mark 12:32:*** *And as God said unto Him, Well, Master,*
> *thou has said the truth, for there is one god,*
> *and there is none other but He.*

> ***Mark 12:33:*** *And to love Him with all the heart*
> *and with all the understanding and with all the soul,*

*and with all the strength, and to love his neighbor as himself*
*is more than all burnt offerings and sacrifices.*

*Mark 12:34: Jesus answered,*
*Thou are not far from the Kingdom of God.*

This man felt the heartbeat of God's law, and that true obedience comes from the heart. This was pleasing to Jesus. I must, in obedience, please Him. If I do not, I am not There.

An in-and-out-of-season prayer of faith life, and a deep relationship with God, makes it easy for us to love Him and all of His offspring – as He wills.

If I cannot love Him; if I cannot love my sisters and brothers in a way of strengthening them spiritually, mentally and physically, I am not There. The There of God's initiated, commanded plan.

Jesus said, When thou art converted, strengthen thy brethren.

Jesus proved His love for us by dying to redeem us. What a kinsman redeemer! It was not just for then, but forever. He made it possible for us to forever be with Him.

We need to search while asking, Do our outer and inner actions demonstrate the love that the Bible speaks about? Deep-rooted, unconditional, agape love – roots in God cannot be uprooted by the enemies.

*Ephesians 3:17: That thirst may dwell in your hearts by faith*
*that you being rooted and grounded in love.*

Hearts where Jesus is welcome contain love. If I do not have Jesus dwelling in my heart, I do not have affectionate, tender feelings with love grounded in Him. I am not There.

*Song of Solomon 8:6:* *Set me a seal upon thine heart*
*as a seal upon thine arm, for love is strong as death.*

*Song of Solomon 8:7:* *Many waters cannot quench love,*
*neither can the flood drown it.*
*If a man would give all the substance of his house for love,*
*it would utterly be despised.*

If I do not have love that will withstand floods, fire, bad times, as well as pleased times, when the umbrella opens to cover and protect, I will not be There.

As time marches me to judgment, I should seek to grow stronger spiritually, developing an even deeper love for God, knowing of His love and patience for me.

Let us entreat the Lord to touch our hearts. Only God's power with our will can give us what it takes to love as He does. If I do not allow Him to fortify me with what it takes, I am not There.

God's love is unconditional, even during our inconsistencies and weaknesses. Yet, he loves us, no matter what we have done, or are doing. Also, He is a non-respecter of person God, whether young, old, sick, well, high or low. Because of His love, He created a salvation for His offspring such that, if we accept, though we have to reap what we have sown, we can still repent and live in His will of love. To be fortified with His love and strength means to be enriched with His agape love, a love that will hold fast through best and worst times. There will be a patrol of it, with enough strength and elasticity to reach God and any individual, race, rich or poor, well and unwell. Many things, even love, I am unable to obtain. Many things, I am unable to give, even love. But, through Jesus, anything is obtainable and demonstrable, even love.

*Mark 12:42: The poor widow threw in two mites. Her all, that was from her heart and free will.*

If it wasn't love which led her, Jesus wouldn't have honored her deed. Giving out her needs was a demonstration of love and concern.

If I do not go beyond my needs; if I do not go beyond the comfort zone, in God's vineyard, to praise and worship Him – to win souls – to administer to needs of my sisters and brothers with love and concern, I am not There.

*Galatians 5:14: For all the law is fulfilled in one word. The word is love. The love of God, rooted and grounded.*

Though this is questioned, how can this be? One word covers all. Yes, it does, because, if we possess the love of Jesus, we will adhere to all of the necessities initiated by Jesus. Without the love of God, it is impossible.

By fellowshipping in a strong, intimate relationship with Jesus, a Godly relationship with His offspring elicits a broad love flow, on which flows caring, sharing, giving – also, wills to sorrow and weep, rejoice and pray, with and for each other.

I need to be consistent in all of these. I need to reexamine my heart, to see if I really care for others, their needs, spiritually, mentally and physically, financially, and for their safety. If I am not diligent in all, I am not There.

> ***John 11:33:*** *When Jesus therefore saw her weeping and the Jews also weeping, which came with Him, He groaned in the spirit, and was troubled.*

My brethren and sisters, what a prime example. Jesus groaned in the spirit, which was a weeping spirit. He was troubled. He became uncomfortable with her. What an effectual demonstration of love, concern and support. Her brothers and sisters supported her. What an effectual example. They wept with her; they were burden-bearers.

There is a need for God's offspring to be robed with this Jesus love and concern. If I am not, I am not There.

*For each, be a leaning post.*

*May evil winds that blow to chill love*

*Become as chaff, blown by the winds of God*

*So that love amongst us be as a humble dove*

*For each be a leaning post anchored with the love rod.*

Let us beseech God for restoration of love. Love as it used to be – as initiated by God. Love has grown cold. In some families, love grew cold when elders departed this life. The fire for God's love was lost. Their offspring busied themselves mostly with fleshly desires.

***Matthew 24:12:*** *Because of iniquity, shall love wax cold.*

The chill of it lodges in families, sanctuaries, the church, the streets and workplaces. There are spirits of disunity. Where there is no sharing in love and peace in earthly homes, and other places here, there will be no sharing in the heavenly home because of the atmosphere here. The atmosphere There is not set up to inherit a kingdom of non-love atmosphere.

If I operate in the non-love/non-sharing atmosphere here, I am not There.

If I live in God's will of love, I shall inherit the benefits He has for His offspring.

I watched my mom's life; she bubbled with love for Jesus, and His offspring, no matter what they were or weren't. It was not always easy for her to demonstrate that love, but she did. A charitable person was she; portraying such love. 1Corinthians 13:3 and 13 says, "And though I bestow all of my goods to feed the poor, and though I give my body to be burned, and have not charity, it profiteth me nothing, and now abideth faith, hope, charity; these three, but the greatest of these is charity."

Jesus loved us so, He hung on the cross to redeem us.

True love demonstrations are not always easy; sometimes, it is costly in energy, time, mental exertion, pain and/or money.

> ***Romans 12:9:*** *Let love be without dissimilation; abhor that which is evil. Cleave to that which is good.*

Even if I have the authority to mistreat, I would not be justified. If I imposed injustice, when there is a need to demonstrate love and care, I need to go above evil to do so; thus, obeying God's law as initiated by Him.

In I Corinthians 13, Paul said, "Though I speak with tongues of angels, have the gift of prophecy, understand all mysteries, all knowledge and have all faith, so that I could move mountains and have not charity (love), I am nothing. Bestow all my goods to feed the poor; give my body to be burned, and have not charity, it profiteth me nothing."

I have always had a giving spirit; but, if I do not possess that agape love and all it takes to be There, then I am not There.

Paul was speaking of love. Charity is love.

> ***Galatians 5:14:*** *For all of the law is fulfilled in one word. Even in this thou shall love thy neighbor as thyself.*

As the people of Israel were reminded of the charge Moses had,

*Joshua 22:5:* *To love the Lord your God,*
*and to walk in all His ways,*

So is Paul reminding us. So is Matthew 5:44: Love your enemies. By loving and praying for my enemies, I can overcome evil with good. I need to love, not only the people of my household and others who love me in return, but those who do not love me, who don't give me anything and talk about me. In doing so – I portray Jesus, letting the world see that He is in me. If I throw stones for stones, I am not There.

Love is the Word; and more important than spiritual gift, love is total.

In the 15th Chapter of Luke, it was love that moved the father to receive his prodigal son back home, even after he had broken the law by asking for his share too soon so he could leave home to live a riotous life. Still, his father did a type of Jesus act, a lasting, unconditional love he demonstrated.

Loving those who have wronged us, praying for them, helping them, and not looking for anything in return – that is to administer to their spiritual, mental and physical needs. There is a great need for spiritual help for soul-saving. God loves this; there is great rejoicing in Heaven when one enters the savings plan. I am charged to help bring that joy. Do people see love demonstrated in and out of me in the home church's house and elsewhere? Do they see a type of Jesus through my love for them? Jesus commanded His disciples to love one another as He loved them. Let awareness of God's love encourage us to love. The inner man needs to be examined, making sure that the love we claim to have is pure and not infamous, but rather the agape love that Jesus speaks about, a love with action and tenderness.

And not only a short, emotional feeling – let it be the love that is fit to enter into God's Kingdom.

> ***John 3:16:*** *For God gave His only begotten son that whosoever believe in Him should not perish, but have everlasting life.*

What love!

> ***Romans 8:39:*** *Nor height nor depth nor any other creature shall be able to separate me from the love of God.*

If I am likely to be separated from the love of God, I am not There. Even though I claim to be. Even though I witness telling of grace and salvation, handing out material on such in various places while traveling, abiding, or while on the street ministry, as I sold nutritious hand-prepared food to benefit the church's house and to lighten the pastor's financial burden – if I do not possess the agape love, I am not There.

Although, I handed material of God's plan, in foreign countries – told of His plan: England, France, Germany, The Bahamas, Jamaica and Canada, and many places inside the U.S.A.

I rode in luxurious vehicles, some from our son's dealership; many have I driven and owned – lodged in beautiful homes of the children, where the best of food was and still is being prepared, all provided by the Greater Than Great God – traveled, dined and shopped with sons, their wives, daughters, their husbands, and with their children.

If my heart is too hard to have and obtain Godly love, and demonstrate it at home and/or abroad – a love that moves me to want not only God's riches for them in this world, but more so for them in the eternal world, then I'm not There. Therefore, I must voice His will, which is an open entrance to soul-saving. I must tell them, do not only look to and ask God to have mercy on their souls, but to have mercy on their own souls by doing what God says it takes for soul-saving. Relentlessly telling them that, no matter how bad this world situation is, or how useless they may think themselves to be, or because of transgressions, God still loves them. (God hates the sin, but loves each of His offspring, and wants them in His saving plan.) Because of His love, salvation is theirs. If they want it. How they can become His trustworthy offspring – how it was made possible on the cross by the kinsredeemer Jesus! Who was resurrected with all power – that He is not dead; He is alive! He rose with power, which He wills to impart to all.


*Romans 8:35: Who shall separate us from the love of Christ,*
*shall tribulation or distress or persecution, or famine,*
*or nakedness, or perils or swords?*

My answer is, no. If my perception is yes, then I am not There.

I need to entreat the Lord to instill in me a heart full of Godly love, fortified with tenderness, void of offenses, working no ills to prevent discards, or anything that transgresses God's law. I want to ever be saturated with love! Love to richly share through His amazing grace's power – His Holy Ghost power.

*When I encounter heartache strife*

*I am never alone in the struggle*

*Because Jesus' love graces my life*

*His love is greater than any trouble.*

**Romans 5:5:** *The love of God is shed abroad in our hearts by the Holy Ghost. Never too deep, wide, or high to caress His offspring, it covers the whole universe.*

There is a height in God that doesn't mean tallness, but a sanctified awesome height of His will. There, where ones who are called by His name should be – a God-initiated place, housed in God's love, grace, mercy and peace – a place where soul-saving salvation reigns, where we need to be; where we need to remain until Jesus' reach. We who endure shall reign with Him in eternal There.

Having the Holy Ghost provides power to love with choices and action. Some confuse the word "love" with different meanings, feelings and actions. The love that God speaks about is a flame that remains kindled in our hearts.

*I John 2:10:* *He that loveth his brother abideth in the light.*

*I John 4:8:* *He that loveth not knoweth not God,*
*for God is love.*

His umbrella of love reaches and covers way out. God's love spreads as fire. Oh, I want to house that fire. In and outside of me, I want that fire aflame. We should all desire to have and keep that flame aglow. Let us beseech the Lord to endow us with that fired flame, for men, women, boys and girls to see and be affected by its warmth. If we love God, we will love everyone; God's love is conducive to loving all – true altruistic love.

*Hebrews 13:1:* *Let brotherly love continue.*

Continue kindness towards those in prison, those who are mistreated, deep sympathetic love. Over and over, Jesus talked about love. He loved with a passion; that is why He redeemed us through suffering. If we do not have God's agape love, we are not There.

# Joy

The joy of the Lord is our strength. The joy of the Lord surpasses regular happiness; it is spiritually delightful. The oil of His joy is wholesome enough to fortify spiritually, mentally and physically, thus promoting healing – not only for the mind and cells, but also spiritual healing of transgressions and iniquities and rebelliousness. To obtain this joy is to be There – God's initiated There.

If we are where we should be in the Lord, we are enriched with His oil of joy that satisfies us to live in His will; letting us know that it is a joyous occasion to live under the shadows of His wings, with hope to inquire in His secret tabernacle, to praise and worship Him; to be commissioned by Him, strengthened by Him. Earthly, nutritious oils don't compare to God's oil of joy.

*Nehemiah 8:10:* *Neither be ye sorry for the joy of the Lord is your strength.*

He does not want only to mediate, but to be magnified by His joyful presence. Our delight is in the law of the Lord. There are so many joyful benefits for those who keep the law of the Lord. He will put gladness in the hearts. Inward joy rebuts sadness; happiness is for a short time, but the joy of the Lord is lasting. If we do not have the joy of the Lord, we are not There.

*Psalms 16:11: Thou will show me the path of life.*
*In thy presence is fullness of joy:*
*at thy right hand there are pleasures forever more.*

If we stay in that place, His pleasures are ours forever.

*Psalms 30:5: In His favor is life.*
*Weeping may endure for a night,*
*but joy cometh in the morning.*

Even when darkness invades with trials and tribulations, I must look towards that beautiful situation, joy in the morning!

*Psalms 51:12: Restore unto me the joy of salvation.*
*Uphold me with thy free spirit.*

My beloved sisters and brethren, let no inequity hamper the joy of the Lord. Remember the Word, while rebuking robbers of joy. Be bold. The Lord is your boast. Be constantly reminded of this.

I have been misused, mistreated, verbally persecuted. I weep, have wept and mourned; have toiled day and night. But the Lord held me up. Joy came on the wings of His mercy, caressed and filled me in due time. I reaped in joy.

**Psalms 126:5:** *They that sow in tears shall reap in joy.*

My tears fall in fertile soil, germinate, spring up and produce joy; therefore, in joy, I reap joy because of God's mercy.

Psalms 126:6 says, "He that goeth forth and weepeth bearing precious seeds shall doubtless come again with rejoicing, bringing his sheaves with him."

This is the word of the Lord: He that goeth forth – if I am not willing to go forth, I am not There.

"Let not the Lord alone," a saying revealed to me while I was still a young wife.

Behold, a vaporous cloud ascended from eastward, appearing on my left and front as I traveled eastward in a narrow path. Out of the cloud, a spiritual hand extended to hand me a large, white envelope. I reached, unafraid, with my right hand. I opened the sealed envelope; inside was a folded, white sheet. I unfolded it; thereon were writings in bold black. My eyes beheld a written charge – "Tell people – let not the Lord alone."

Though I am mistreated or persecuted, because I am being obedient to the charge, I will not stop. I must beseech the Lord for help in telling people to not let the Lord alone. I shall not compromise. Under the coverage of His blood, robed in His coat of armor, surrounded by His hedge of thorns, mercy and grace, I must persevere in His joy. In His fear, I must obey and not listen to voices of persecutors.

> *Isaiah 50:10: Who is among you that feareth the Lord,*
> *that obeyeth the voice of His servant,*
> *that walketh in darkness and hath no light?*
> *Let him trust in the name of the Lord, and stay upon his God.*

If I disobey my God, listening to voices of the persecuting enemies, I am not There.

> *Isaiah 51:11: Therefore the redeemed of the Lord shall return and come with singing unto Zion, and everlasting joy shall be upon their head. They shall obtain gladness and joy, and sorrow and mourning shall flee away.*

Surely, this joy comes from a sure walk in God. This joy is awesome! It shuns away sorrow, heartaches and other pains.

> *John 16:20: Your sorrow shall be turned into joy.*

In the strength of this joy, I will worship. I will praise Him with this joy, which is obtainable through the power of God Omnipotent. I shall continue praying for the joy of others near and all over this world. No, not for the joy bred from lust, eating, drugs, alcohol, and other sin and health damagers; but the joy of our Creator God Omnipotent.

**Philippians 1:4:** *Paul prayed for the Philippians with joy.*

This encourages me to pray with joy and gladness for my pastor, his household, sisters and brethren – also, the fruits of my womb, seeds of their earthly father; also, their households. I pray that my prayer in the image of a bird is used by God Omniscient to bring this joy to all, along with other needs there are, even places and situations.

I pray that God helps others and me to succumb to His will with joy, even in these times when the spirit of complacency is prevalent. If I do not succumb with joy to His will, I am not There.

And, though I witness telling of God's plan everywhere I go or abide; though I speak in the heavenly language, praying, praising and worshipping God, going to sanctuaries both night and day – if I am not where I need to be in the Lord, I am not There. I see being There as being in the will of God – in His plan – living it, and growing in it.

Having all fruits of the spirit knitted inside of me; operating faithfully, with one accord, in God's will, each demonstrating each of their built-in Godly attributes, which are beckoning lights for drawing men, women, boys and girls.

I must embrace all, even the commandment which I beseech the Lord to engrave on the table of my heart and mind.

And, if I should falter, falling short of some or just one depicts absenteeism from the place; that, when I fall short of just one, ineligibility takes place; therefore, I no longer qualify to be in that place, There.

That is when I need to fall on my face, in deep repentance, to the Lord, seeking His forgiveness and restoration in Jesus' name; and to be stabilized by deep roots in Him, to not be uprooted when various tempestuous winds of evil blow. Yes, I really need to grab and hold onto the horns of the altar.

**John 16:24:** *Hitherto have you asked nothing in my name: ask and ye shall receive that your joy may be full.*

**Philippians 2:2:** *Fulfill ye my joy.*

Even though God has it to give, it may not be given, because I did not entreat Him with faith prayer. It is a sin not to pray.

If I do not pray always, I am not There.

I must continue, so that His joy remains in me. There must be a consistency.

**John 15:11:** *(Jesus speaking)*
*These things have I spoken unto you,*
*that my joy may remain in you,*
*and that your joy might be full.*

The joy of communicating and having a deep relationship with Him is conducive to keeping one focused and alert, and produces zeal to keep on keeping on.

If I am where I should be in the Lord, being obedient, He will enrich me with this joy, even when situations make it seem impossible. All is possible with God. This joy is only of the Lord; therefore, I need to have the Greater Than Great inside of me (Jesus).

I am looking for a kingdom, but I must do what it takes to get, and inhabit, the place There. I am not looking for kingdom here; I am looking for a kingdom over There, one not yet seen. In the joy of the Lord, I look. I must not overlook the cross, but take it up to bear in the joy of the Lord, praising Him for the resurrection, the rising of Our Lord Jesus from the dead. Yes, Jesus, our kinsman redeemer. Not only in sanctuaries, but other places, at all times – yes, delightfully in my soul, I shall bless the Lord. I beseech Him for strength to persevere. In Jesus' name, I ask, and shall continue asking. I want to be and remain faithful, being His trustworthy offspring.

*Matthew 25:21: Thou good and faithful servant, thou has been faithful over a few things. I will make thee ruler over many things: Enter. Enter thou into the joy of the Lord.*

Where He enters me, I want to stay There and bloom. What beautiful and appealing blooms those will be, enriched with the joy of the Lord.

If I am There, where God wills me to be, I shall be saturated with the blessing of His gorgeousness. Therefore, if I am not in God's will, I am not There.

# Peace

Also, being There is peace. The peace that surpasses all. Webster defines "peace" as freedom from or a stopping of war; freedom from public disturbances. All of the above refers to secular peace. But, the peace that is about to be read about is conducive to all the fruits of the spirit, and is the inner peace of God, which no mortal is able to give . . . a peace which is viable to humbleness.

That inner peace can be obtained from the Lord by being There – There, where He wills – to have a will to house that peace, and allow the peace light to shine while practicing peace and endeavoring to be honest towards all. To be a promoter of peace is pleasing to God, and promotes a healthy, Godly environment.

Three times, Isaac dug wells—for the two first wells, the Philistines filled with dirt. This hindered the flow of water; therefore, their work was in vain.

For peace's sake, Isaac did not fight back; he did not exercise vengeance. Instead, he and his servants moved on and dug wells the third time. All of God's offspring who are called by His name should flee confusion, as Isaac did.

We need to ask God for wisdom and knowledge in knowing when to retreat and when to fight. No other directs like God. Without God's means, it is easy to retrogress to turmoil, Had Isaac retrogressed to turmoil, hurt and pain would have come to his servants – and family – even though they were innocent in the beginning.

In God is peace and progress.

So, Isaac found peace and much blessing in God, because he resolved conflicts – which was an exchange for peace; also, an act of obedience to his Lord. He pressed on to all of the blessings God had for him.

*Tell about the love of Jesus*

*Let this be told near and far*

*His mercy, grace and peace for us*

*Whether in peace or in war.*

Satan uses different snares to rob us of peace to bring strife. The scripture says we are not to be ignorant of Satanic devices.

**II Corinthians 2:11:** *Lest Satan should get an advantage of us, for we are not ignorant of his devices, let us focus on God's promise for peace.*

If I react to injustice, seeking vengeance, I am not There. Obedience to God leads to local and national peace. One main ingredient for peace is obedience to God, Number

One. Better than sacrifice, peace is one of the fruits of the spirit.

*Psalms 34:14:* *Depart from evil and do good;*
*seek peace and pursue it –*

means to search for it, pant for it, absorb it with a willing hunger of want. Ask God to deeply implant the spirit pf peace within, to forever stay and be magnified for His glory.

That is why it is so crucial that we are filled with the Holy Ghost, for that "within" peace. The Holy Ghost and peace are all in Him (Jesus). Jesus gives satisfying peace to each who love and obey Him.

*I John 4:4:* *Greater is he that is in me*
*than he that is in the world.*

My sisters and brothers, being filled with the Holy Ghost, I need to be careful not to sow discord, breeding confusion. If I do not eschew evil, if I do not live and model peace, by not reaping vengeance, by my attitude, walk or my tongue, even when others are for confusion, persecution, even war, still I need to exercise peace with my will, enforced by the strength of God.

*Psalms 120:7:* *I am for peace, but when I speak,*
*they are for war.*

I need to pray that warriors, persecutors and confusers get in Jesus' plan and become peacemakers. This is pleasing to God. They, too, are God's offspring, needing to repent. God loves them. He loves us all. Many things we do, or do not do, He does not love. We all fall short of His glory. The Bible succinctly tells us to pray for those who misuse us. With my mind seeking oneness with the mind of God, prayer is one of the greatest privileges, not only for peace, but for all necessities – for being There. In writings, and from my tongue and lips, I ask God to let my prayers be world-wide, and for Him to use as He sees needed. Yes, Lord, from me, your servant.

**Psalms 122:6:** *Pray for peace of Jerusalem.*

David was not asking for prayers to bring peace to him-self, but for his sisters and brothers – interceding for them, as I and others need to do for others, that they may be blessed with peace, both spiritually and mentally – not only to avoid secular conflicts, but to bow in repentance, seeking to save their souls with true repentance. To enter and live in God's plan is a deep-seated "within" peace, one of the main ingredients for a closer walk with the Master. There is no peace as the peace of Jesus.

**John 14:27:** *Jesus told His disciples, Peace I leave with you; my peace, I give unto you, not as the world giveth peace.*

Peace is one among the many blessed benefits that the world cannot give – and, in a lot of areas, do not want to, even if it was possible. In fact, in most cases – well, I should say the people in the world, for it is the people in the world, the evil spirits, the principalities and the flesh of men, women, boys and girls that ignites turmoil; the very opposite of peace, not wanting God's servants to have peace. There is a failure to understand that, even in the midst of it all, there is a peace of God; that is peace in valleys, as well as on mountain heights. Through faith, I enjoy this peace. If our quality of life is acceptable for God's There, His peace is in us – deeply rooted – if we allow it to be. Surely in the Holy Ghost we shall obtain and maintain this joyous peace, not of this world. If I do not have this peace, I am not There.

**Romans 5:** *Being justified by faith, we have peace with God through our Lord Jesus Christ.*

Peace with God differs from the feeling of calmness. Peace with God means that we are reconciled with God. There is no blockage. This peace is number one.

Some believe that it is impossible to obtain and maintain peace. Not so. God made it possible. If I do not have it, it is no one's fault but mine. Peace inside of me should penetrate, touch, God and others; having peace with God, and His offspring.

I must let the peace of God rule in my heart, not be a warrior of strife; the absence of peace brings jeopardy to oneself – non-satisfactory, constant complaining; strife, nega-tiveness; spiritual, mental and physical – chronic diseases.

Lack of peace hinders prayers from being heard and an-swered; hinders communication with not only God, but with offspring also and could hinder earthly prosperities made possible by God. Storm from lack of peace creates ominous strife to affect its carrier and/or others.

I need and must be willing to let God help me select the best rule choice for the rule of peace. My will, swallowed in by His will, brings sweet peace, with sleepful nights – away from a life of frustration and stagnation. I want my overall vision and attitude to be focused on things of the Lord Eter-nal. Oh, I want to be in His spiritual reign – There.

# Longsuffering

If I want to please God, I must also be a longsufferer. What does the word "longsuffering" mean?

Webster says: bearing injuries, insults, troubles, patiently, for a long time; endurance of trials. But, God did not put a time limit. He wants us to be forever longsufferers (dying to self).

A certain writer wrote:

When you are forgotten, or neglected, or purposely set at naught, and you do not sting or hurt with the insult or oversight, but your heart is happy, being counted worthy to suffer for Christ, you are dying to self.

When your good is evil spoken of, when your wishes are crossed, your advice is disregarded, your opinions ridiculed, and you refuse to let anger rise in your heart or even defend yourself; but you take it all with patience and loving silence, you are dying to self.

When you lovingly and patiently bear disorder, irregularity, unpunctuality or annoyance; when you stand face to face with waste, folly, extravagance, spiritual insensibility and endure it as Jesus endured, you are dying to self.

To endure longsuffering, being able to die to self, as listed by the writer, one must stay prayerful, keeping eyes on Jesus. Prayer will not stop temptation, but will prevent yielding. We cannot prevent fowls from flying overhead, but we can prevent them from resting on our heads. If I want to be a longsufferer, pleasing to God, I shall always beseech him for what it takes to be one.

*Jeremiah 33:3: Call unto me and I will answer thee,*
*and shew thee great and mighty things,*
*which thou knowest not.*

Knowing that He is a bearer of any weight, I must be willing to withstand pain and distress while looking through the eyes of faith to the bearer of bearers, Jesus. If I do not, I am not There. And knowing that each inflicted burden, pain or unjust treatment, if demonstrated in longsuffering – enduring without complaining – sets one in a higher realm in God's reign; if I do not step-by-step reach higher levels in Him, working in His plan with a willing, made-up mind of a high tolerance strength, diligently gathering sheaves while avoiding confusion, standing on His word, holding onto His promise under any circumstance; receiving His charge, keeping it, and looking through the eyes of faith, I am not There.

His word is Truth. His word provides solidness for endurance, a product of longsuffering. If I am not a longsufferer, I am not a candidate for the promise.

**Hebrews 6:15:** *And so after he had patiently endured, he obtained the promise.*

For, obtaining the spirit of longsuffering, it takes patience to endure, as Abraham had.

Even though someone does me wrong, I must not seek vengeance. I've got to die to self. If I do, I am being disobedient to God, because He plainly said that, "Vengeance is mine." Also, if I did, I would be doing what He is supposed to do; therefore, He cannot do it, for I would have tied his hands for me to mess up things, bringing reproach. Conversely, I need to forgive and pray, asking God to change wrongdoers into what He wills them to be – save their souls.

Jesus did not condemn the woman caught in adultery; He forgave her. But, He told her to go and sin no more.

**Matthew 27:12:** *When the priest and elders falsely accused Jesus, He answered nothing. He did not try to defend Himself, fighting back. On the cross He asked forgiveness for the crucifiers. Father forgive them, for they know not what they do.*

My, my! What dying to self! What love, what longsuffering! What a longsuffering example for all of His offspring. I beseech Him to make me more and more as He. Oh, I must, I must, or I am not There.

Having a right relationship with Jesus is knowing that there is strength for endurance, whether in trials, sickness, pain or distress. Yes, in Him, I am equipped for longsuffering. Under the shadows of His wings, I am content with the food, raiment and housing, the climate and all of His attributes. I praise Him for the steps of His salvation. Though, sometimes I am in the discomfort zone, still I am happy in the Lord, the Holy Ghost – inside of me, cease not to comfort, making longsuffering a way of life.

The suffering of longsufferers is rewarding, if done to the glory of the Lord of Lords (Jesus). In them are productive seeds, which don't fall only on infertile soil or stony elements, but many fall on fertile soil – to germinate, spring up, be nourished by God's anointing. They grow and are magnified by His anointing. Their spread is wide. The magnitude of each branch affects who is touched by its tips.

The spirit of a longsufferer is valuable, producing seeds fit to please God. Seeds to produce Godly fruits: love, joy, peace, longsuffering, gentleness, goodness, faith, meekness, temperance, and much more.

With a high tolerance, with patience, I diligently wait on the Lord while avoiding confusion. Yes, waiting on His promise, I look through the eyes of unwavering faith. With all of these attributes, I stand on the Word, the anchor for enduring longsuffering – even when wrong presents itself. I must remain calm. I must die to self, as the stoned Stephen did, I must do. While dying, he asked God to forgive the stoners. What a great forgiver was he, also. If I do not have a forgiving spirit, I am not There.

It has been said, and is still being said, that I am too easy, letting people wrong me. But, as long as I am in the Lord, all is well. Though, sometimes I am short of the glory, still it is in my utmost will to be and operate in His will, for I know that, if I am not in His will, I am not in that place so viable for soul-saving – the place, There.

*Lord My Soul Take*

*As I exhale my last, Lord my soul take*

*To ever be gently alive in your domain*

*And joyful noise from my soul, for your glory, make*

*As the light of your agape love upon my soul reign.*

# Gentleness

Let the power of gentleness in my mind be for distribution to the spirit, who is able to spread it amongst all of God's children.

Many have and are being won by the spirit of fruitful plants from seeds of gentleness that have sprung up, grown and spread, reached and touched others. If they endure and reach There, and remain There, what reaping of blessed rewards there shall be from the hand of the awesome rewarder, Jesus! Praise God! May the overflowing of reward earnings continue in the beauty of gentleness, glorifying the Creator of it all.

Another attribute to being There is operating in the Holy Ghost, who operates to gently comfort us. Most define gentleness as polite, kind, generous, courteous, and gentle. By some, these attributes are used sometimes for certain reasons, gains, etc. After getting what it is they want to obtain or promote, gentleness is laid aside, to be picked up later; to robe the wearer or user, making it easy to pursue or obtain, even swindle, what is desired. So many innocents have been robbed, even murdered, by those possessed by wolves' spirits, garbed in gentle sheep's clothing. Truly, this is not the gentleness that God created and speaks about.

His gentleness does not impose hurt, heartaches, downgrading oppression, non-respecter of person or robbery – seeking gain from innocents as grievous wolves.

His gentleness is a built-in, non-begrudging, calm, operating love affair – a love that lifts and props the weak, a love that makes the strong stronger.

I need to operate, not as a wolf in sheep's clothing, but rather garbed in the will of God, brave as a lion, humble as a dove; praying always to remain applying this to all aspects of life; moving from feet to head. First, gentle attitude, spirit, body language, focus, walk and expressions – non-disruptive and loud. Gentleness plays a crucial part in the Kingdom of God; is generous – kind, not harsh or rude.

It is a blessing to be gentle. It is a blessing to have a vision of it, though most visions are for appointed times. Visions of God's will shall speak and not lie; though it tarry, wait faithfully for it. Surely, it will come to pass. The vision for gentleness is for now and the future, to be used at all times among God's offspring.

> **I Thessalonians 2:7:** *But we were gentle among you, even as a nurse cheereth her children.*

True gentleness uplifts, with a non-respecter of person attitude.

Let gentleness utter its voice through a blessed horn, soothing to all ears and minds. Gentleness is kind; its fruits are suitable to use as a balming salve for souls, or food for the healing of mind, through the power of God. Why through His power? Because gentleness is one of the fruits of the spirit initiated by Him. If I do not operate with gentleness, I am not There.

**Psalms 18:35:** *David said,*
*And thy gentleness hath made me great.*

Many believe that gentleness only brings greatness, a combination of opportunities, talents and earthly gains. But pure greatness comes from being in God's will, and acknowledging that it is through God's gentleness and mercy that we reap true blessings and abilities.

**II Samuel 22:36:** *Thou hast also given me*
*the shield of salvation, and thy gentleness has made me great;*
*thou hast enlarged my steps under me, so that my feet did not*
*slip.*

These words are in a song of David's to the Lord. In tribulation, if I lean on the Lord, having a gentle spirit, I am allowing Him to show forth His power; I am allowing His glory to shine. I must let gentleness be embedded with calm love from a sincere heart, unbegrudgingly. I must let the power of gentleness be in the core of my mind for distribution to my spirit, to spread among the brethren and sisters, even among wrongdoers or the unlearned, concerning the Word of God. Let gentleness draw them to God's plan. I must sow seeds of gentleness. In doing so, fruit-bearing plants shall burst forth, spring up, and grow into fruit-bearing plants pleasing to God, the Rewarder – Glory to His name. The overflowing gentleness shall flow and level into the beauty of peace in the brightness of God's light. If I do not possess that flowing gentleness, I am not There.

Gentleness is not rude; it allows, allowing each to express oneself. It listens and responds with kindness, meeting needs; has a gentle attitude, in and away from home or the church's home – out of the pastor's presence, or others in authority – approaching and responding with a lamb-like spirit, not loud or rude. Let gentleness rule in spirits' minds, hearts and attitudes. Let it rule in looks, talk and walk – with satisfaction, saturated with the oil of joy.

One who operates in gentleness has the character of a well-named gentleman, or gentlewoman, pleasing to God, whose gentleness is faithful, kind, meek and uplifting.

*I Corinthians 2:3: Paul speaking:*
*I was with you in weakness and fear, and much trembling.*

True gentleness is equipped with what it acquires to help those who are weak and fearful, the lost and unlearned. There is a need to promote friendship with a sympathetic warmth in the torch of gentleness. Gentleness ignites to a higher realm in God's vineyard, with an effective spirit amongst

God's offspring, bringing in fruits for repentance – not with self-pride and glory, or swollen with self-righteousness, but glorifying God, who is the owner of all.

If I do not praise God for His gentleness, I do not possess gentleness that glorifies Him, being gentle to His offspring, I am not There.

For all of this, I need Godly wisdom and strength, because it is all of Him.

*James 3:17: James' Epistle to the Twelve:*
*For the wisdom from above is pure then peaceable,*
*gentle and easy to be entreated.*
*Full of mercy and good fruits without part*
*– partiality, without hypocrisy.*

*We need to be spiritually fructified bearing much in the vineyard of the Lord*

*Having much fruit sense of non-slothful, but having perseverance*

*Being fruitful in and out of season; being fruitful in drawing rewards*

*When Jesus comes to deliver, we shall be happy for his appearing*

Oh, I want to be in that assigned place of God. When I am called, I want to be in God's will, of none striving.

*II Timothy 2:24: And the servant of the Lord must not strive,*
*but be gentle to all men apt to teach with patience.*

I am a servant of God, but I cannot be There by doing only part of His will. I must do all of His will, while producing spiritual fruits, with gentleness. If I do, I am There. If I do not, I am not There.

# Goodness

To be There, one needs to produce goodness, another fruit of the spirit.

Webster defines goodness as the "state or quality of being good; excellence, kindness, generosity." One who possesses these qualities as God's will pities and unselfishly helps another, or others; is mild-tempered, not easily angered or annoyed, free-willed with a kind and friendly attitude; operating in willingness, honorable and worthy, not looking for pay in return – knowing that God is the rewarder.

*Exodus 34:6: The Lord God merciful and gracious, longsuffering and abundant in goodness and truth.*

I need to see the goodness of the Lord, and be happy in it.

I cannot claim by work or merit to be good in God's sight. The state or quality of being good doesn't apply to the offspring of God. The Bible says there is none good but God; still, by His power, if I allow, He will produce goodness through me – possessing a cheerful, agreeable attitude; kind, tender-hearted, say as Paul the Apostle said, "There is no good thing in me. But I can produce good fruit through Him." Being able to see goodness about others, the top priority of our spirit, should be to do good. This is possible if we are willing and living as God wills. It is a good thing to be filled with the Holy Ghost. It does not only lead and guide, but also comforts and strengthens. We shall be strong and comfortable while being led by the Holy Spirit, to do good with God's love working through us; goodness is produced in us. Without God, there are no good things in us. It is an enrichment to have Him working inside of our life. We have to want and accept Him to produce goodness through us.

Though I try to do good, do right, and be just, still the only good life pleasing to Jesus is to have a close relationship of His will, being nourished by Him, bearing much fruit. In Him, I have my boast. Of myself, there is no boast, because it's all in Him.

*Psalms 52:1: Why boasteth thyself in mischief,*
*oh mighty man?*

*Psalms 52:1: The goodness of the Lord endureth forever.*

Doeg saw himself as great, boasting about his deeds. As many others, he confused his accomplishments with goodness, which was displeasing to God. He should have given the honor to God, measuring what he did by the rule of God's word. It is God who gives understanding to man.

If I fail to honor God for accomplishments, as Doeg did, I am not There.

I must tell of the goodness of the Lord – His mighty deeds, and all that He does for me.

**Psalms 145:7:** *They shall abundantly utter the memory of thy great goodness, and shall sing of thy righteousness.*

The Psalm says, "Thou crowneth the year with thy goodness, thy path drops fatness."

His goodness is so rich, so much so that it drops fatness. I have no excuse. How can I miss His goodness? I pant for Him to anoint me with it, to His glory. If I possess such goodness, I will bear fruits of such goodness, which will be portrayed characteristically with the love of He who ordained goodness. I shall approach my fellowmen with the spirit of Godly goodness. I need to depend faithfully on God for creating the right spirit inside of me, for producing goodness pleasing to Him. With His goodness inside of me, it will flow and caress – even to benefit others.

**Matthew 5:16:** *Let your light shine before me that they may see your good works.*

We know that God is good, better than good! He is awesome. His law is, too. We need to use it lawfully, bearing fruits of goodness.

### *Psalms 33:5:* *He loveth righteousness and judgment.*

The earth is full of the goodness of God. It is for us to behold and obtain His goodness, and shed abroad; and spend less time in worldly escapades. Allow His goodness to be stayed in our spirits and minds, while utilizing beneficial ways to glorify Him. Lead the lost to His Word. His goodness endureth forever. If I do not spread goodness among others, I am not There.

I have a burning desire to be in God as I need to, living a life pleasing to Him. That is why I keep reaching each day and night, asking Him to endow me within and out, with what it takes to be. For I know this; that, if I am not where I ought to be, how do I expect to be in that designated place of His? How can I expect Him to hear and answer my prayers? Oh, how I do not want to praise, worship, or call Him in vain. I want to live, so that my prayers are eligible to be heard and answered. He is a just and holy God. My prayers need to be sent out from a clean heart, clean tongue, and lips endowed by the Holy Ghost.

I ask Him for all that I voice to Him, bless me with a voice pleasing to Him, enriched with His anointing – a voice with sounds of many waters, if He wills. Truly, I do not want to not be eligible to inherit the abode He has prepared in yonder's dimension. This, I pray, not only for me, but others, even for the fruits of my womb, seeds of my husband.

I praise God for His blessing upon me, even before concievement, the fashioning in my mother's womb, and the exitation; and the many, many afterwards. I know this, that

I must live for Him, using this body that He made. I must, in loudness, praise Him. He brought me here to have fellowship with Him, praise and worship Him. Therefore, a charge is laid upon me, which, in obedience, through perilous and non-perilous times, I must render. If I do not, I am not There.

I must not only talk about the Lord and His goodness, I must live and walk it, too.

*Romans 2:21:* *Thou therefore which teacheth another, teacheth thou not thyself? Thou that preacheth a man should not steal, dost thou steal?*

Truly, we need to demonstrate what we teach, in and out of the presence of others – even in the dark.

*Romans 12:1:* *I beseech you therefore Brethren, by the mercies of God, that you present your bodies a living sacrifice, wholly acceptable unto God, which is your reasonable service.*

When His righteousness and goodness is proclaimed, we ought to be in a position to witness.

**NOTE:** Oftentimes, when His goodness is mentioned, His righteousness is, also. This should make us aware that it is critical that we should be what we need to be, to obtain the goodness which He is willing to endow us with: right in spirits, minds, looks and issuances – each must accompany all with a fiery zeal.

***Isaiah 63:7:*** *I will mention the loving kindness of the Lord, and the praises of the Lord according to all that the Lord has bestowed on us and the great goodness toward the house of Israel.*

Israel did sin; still, our forgiving God bestowed goodness upon them.

Though, there are no good things in men, except through God's power. He creates goodness inside of me, so that I may glorify Him, and to bless His offspring. I must have a will for Him, to do so. I must fear Him, with love and trust. I need to stay under His umbrella of goodness.

***Psalms 27:13:*** *I had fainted unless I had believed to see the goodness of the Lord in the land of the living.*

We must live in obedience to God's goodness. We must have faith in Him, with thanksgiving, desiring a manifestation of His loving goodness to live inside of us, to always bless others, to constantly lift up the Lord. For, greater than great is the goodness of Him.

***Psalms 31:19:*** *Oh how great is the goodness which thou hast laid up for them that trust in thee before the sons of men!*

God is good all of the time, so He wants us to be. It is not enough to be good some of the time. God has all power; He is able to bring good out of no good. We should beseech

Him, for producing goodness within us. Let us do so with faith and patience, waiting on Him in obedience.

**I Samuel 13:9:** *Rather than wait, Saul offered the sacrifice himself.*

He disobeyed God. He became impatient, and did that which was not in agreement with God's plan.

If we become impatient and do that which is not in agreement with God's plan, we are out of His will; therefore, we are not There. The Bible says obedience is better than sacrifice. We need to obey God. If His goodness is manifested inside of us, then we are able to obey Him. True goodness must come from God into us; it is not what we do of our own fleshly self.

How thankful I am for His unexplainable goodness that is beyond my intellectual ability.

**Exodus 34:6:** *And the Lord passed by before him and proclaimed, the Lord, the Lord God, merciful and gracious, longsuffering, and abundant in goodness and truth.*

**Nehemiah 9:25:** *And so they did eat and were filled and became fat and delighted themselves in the great goodness of God!*

God abounds in goodness; His goodness abounds in mercy. We are blessed by His goodness.

Surely, His goodness and mercy shall follow me all the days of my life.

Even in our failures, He is good in patience. The goodness of the Lord is with us each day and night. What a shame His goodness, His blood, men trample underfoot.

If I do not appreciate His goodness, thanking and praising Him, I am not There.

# Faith

*Hebrews 11:1:* *Now faith is the substance hoped for,*
*the evidence of things not seen.*

Another crucial fruit for being There is faith, which is one
of the fruits of the spirit.

Webster says that faith is "unquestioning belief in God."

To trust.

Mom was often heard saying that faith was belief, or trust
in God. She saw it as an unlocker, repetitiously stressing
that prayer was the key and faith – the unlocker. Mom was
a crying prayer warrior. I, too, perceive faith to be an unlocker; that is, unwavering faith, without doubts and fears,
is an opener, a penetrator, a piercer; is causative, a causer of
requests to God to be heard and answered, producing effects
if the requests are in God's will.

There are good and bad faith.

Good faith – sincerity, honesty, genuine.

Bad faith is insincerity.

Also, I define faith to be much more; that is, genuine faith is a mover, an uprooter, of placid evil and diseases, bringing about healing, a raiser, a deliverer. Prayer is the key, but faith is the unlocker by turning the key. Without the key, closure remains. Prayer without faith is to no avail. Faith causes the unseen to appear. Yes, through God's power, the impossible in the carnal is made possible.

**II Corinthians 5:7:** *For we walk, by faith, not by sight.*

Yes, we must have faith to please God – faith for our prayers to be heard and answered – unquestioning belief in Him. Complete trust and confidence. Confidence, another word my mother defined as faith.

**Mark 11:22:** *Jesus told His disciples to have faith in God.*

**Matthew 9:22:** *Jesus said, Daughter, be of good comfort; thy faith hath made you whole.*

It took faith for her to be healed.

**Luke 7:44:** *Jesus said to the woman who anointed His head with oil and washed His hair with her tears, also kissed His feet, Thy faith hath saved thee. Go in peace.*

Faith saves, faith brings peace. This woman had faith, also demonstrations of faith. Works. Faith without work is dead. It doesn't take much faith. Jesus said faith the size of a mustard seed is sufficient, but must be genuine, unwavering. God has given all a measure of faith, which is crucial that the measure be kept in the spirit of us, His offspring. I need to beseech God for strength for my sisters, brothers, and myself, that the measure faithfully remain. If I do not, I am not There.

*Luke 22:32: Jesus said to His disciples:*
*I have prayed for thee that thou faith fail not;*
*and when thou art converted, strengthen thy brethren.*

Jesus opened the faith door to the gentiles. The faith of God brings increase in the Kingdom of God.

*The Acts 16:5: And so were the churches established*
*in the faith and increased in number daily.*

*Romans 1:17: Therein the righteousness of God revealed*
*from faith to faith: as it is written, the just shall live by faith.*

If I do not live by faith, I am not There.

Faith is total dependence on God, without doubts and fears, which is the opposite of genuine faith. God's hand is tied when doubts and fears appear. Complete trust is needed, with a will to be in His will, complete with humble obedience. Most importantly, it is the sincerity of our faith, not the amount. Doubts and fears kill faith.

When the disciples asked Jesus to increase their faith, He let them know that they only needed a small grain.

I pray God that my faith is strong enough to stand the rigorous trials and persecutions. God is faithful and able to carry me through all. Though Peter denied Jesus, he was forgiven because of a faithful God.

Peter started walking on the water in faith; but, when the wind became boisterous, his faith began to dwindle. Jesus carried him safely over. I must remember that He is the one who is able to increase my faith and deliver me. Sometimes, people who don't claim to be Christians of faith put to shame the ones with stagnant faith, who have received the Holy Ghost.

There are some who don't want to be exposed to God's light, fearing that the darkness in their lives will be exposed. They reject changes.

Beloved sisters and brothers, I need God's light to shine in and out of me, hoping, with prayer of faith, to be purged, making me a drawing light for Jesus. I must search myself to see if I am trusting in me, rather than Jesus, the one of all possibilities. Faith produces dependence on God.

*Mark 9:23:* *Jesus said to the father of the possessed son,*
*If thou canst believe,*
*all things are possible to him that believeth.*

Jesus is saying that anything is possible, if we believe, because nothing is impossible with God. We may not get everything we ask for, or it may not be provided at the time we expect it to be; but, God Omniscient knows what, when and how we need to receive whatever it is that we request. He also knows, for some people to possess or be endowed with certain things brings pride, which results in falls. We need to eschew pride, one of the words on God's hate list.

One thing I do know and have is the opportunity to have everything, to be His faithful trustworthy offspring. My faith must manifest in actions, works. If I profess to have faith, but am not impregnated with faith fruits to be issued, as initiated by the author and finisher of faith, I am barren. Faith without production is dead. I hunger to produce, not for the praise of men, but for the glory and lifting up of Jesus. In obedience, I travail for His strength in production and the bringing forth.

If I do not, I am not There.

Too, we need to take on the shield of faith. Another thing, faith is an all-around shield.

**Ephesians 6:16:** *Above all taking the shield of faith, wherewith ye shall be able to quench all the fiery darts of the wicked.*

Faith is protection from any evil, and has overcoming power.

**II Thessalonians 3:2:** *And that we may be delivered from unreasonable and wicked men, for all men hath not faith.*

For all of this, we truly need unfeigned faith; hold on, never departing from it.

*I Timothy 1:5:* *Charity of a pure heart and of a good conscience and of faith unfeigned to my faith I must add virtue.*

I must persevere, maintaining the faith with boldness, beseeching God to rebuke evil faith-snatchers. We are living in a perilous atmosphere, a falling away one.

*I Timothy 4:1:* *Now the spirit speaketh expressively, that in the latter time, some shall depart from the faith, giving heed to seducing spirits and doctrines of evil.*

By faith, I must beseech God to keep me from being seduced. If I do not, I am not There.

The prayers of faith are viable for answers.

*James 5:15:* *The prayers of faith shall save the sick.*

In my walks for God, I do not want to become a waverer, tossed by winds of doubt and fear.

*James 1:6:* *But let him ask in faith, nothing wavering, for he that wavereth is like a wave of the sea driven with the wind and tossed.*

If I am driven and tossed, I am not fruitful in God's sight. I am of no use to His offspring. How can, being unstable, stand strong to aid or help any needy cause?

I must be deeply rooted in the faith. If I am not, I am not There.

*I Peter 1:7: That the trial of your faith being much more precious than gold that perisheth, though it be tried with fire, might be found unto praise and honor and glory at the appearing of Christ.*

When Jesus appears to exit me, I want to be faithfully ready, with the Holy Ghost within.

*Jude 1:20: For ye beloved building up yourselves in your most holy faith, praying in the Holy Ghost.*

There is power in Holy Ghost praying. I see the Holy Ghost as an anchor for faith, and faith an anchor – carrier of the Holy Ghost.

*Jude 1:21: Looking for the mercy of our Lord Jesus Christ unto eternal life.*

Oh, I want to be in that number, who, with patience, kept the faith, as the Apostle Brother Paul.

If I have not kept the faith, I won't be There.

*II Timothy 4:7: I have fought a good fight. I have finished my course; I have kept the faith. Henceforth, there is laid up for me a crown of righteousness, which the Lord the Righteous Judge shall give me at that day: and not me only, but unto all them also that love His appearing.*

Paul had lived a life of faith; that is why, on the end, he could testify as he did. Faith enriched his walk with God – also, anchored his whole being.

If I endure as Paul, I shall receive victory through Christ. Faith gives me an above view of this world's riches and escapades. Even if I am not rewarded here, I shall be, and live forever, in yonder's land. Yes, after the promised resurrection of my faithful God. I thank Him for the cross and shed blood. Some of the faithful heroes of the Bible were tortured, not accepting deliverance, that they might obtain a better resurrection.

Stephen was a great man of Jesus.

*The Acts 7:59-60: And they stoned Stephen as he was calling upon God, saying, Lord Jesus, receive my spirit; and he knelt down and cried with a loud voice, Lord, lay not this sin to their charge; and when he had said this, he fell asleep.*

A faithful servant with a forgiving spirit – truly, he was There, doing God's will in His vineyard.

When I am scorned and laughed at for doing God's will in faith, I am not discouraged. I must remain faithful inwardly, as well as outwardly, allowing faith to affect others. If I do not remain faithful, I am not There.

When my goodliness is evil spoken of, my desires unmet, my opinion ridiculed; if I am not angered, not trying to defend myself, and in my patience remain silent, I died to self.

If I am persecuted for Jesus' sake means I am being faithful. The faithful shall be rewarded when God enters them into His Kingdom, where no persecution is. I may lose friends, even the life called mine, which is His. But, the eternal life can no man or principalities take. By faith, I shall let no one hinder me from that destiny.

*We Need God*

*The adversary wants us to lose faith in our Lord.*

*We do good to resist him with prayer and trusting*

*With boldness, against the forces with one accord*

*And stay on our God who is a deliverer, everlasting.*

Lack of faith causes problems, not only with God directly, but with His creations, man, etc. Also, waiting on God is faith. To wait is also patience. If I cannot wait on God, I am not There.

**Genesis 16:3:** *And Sarai, Abram's wife,*
*took Hagar her maid the Egyptian,*
*and gave her to her husband Abram, to be his wife,*
*so she could obtain a child by her.*

Because of a lack of faith, Sarai did not wait on the promise given by God, saying that she, Sarai, would bear a son.

Because of the lack, there arose problems during that time. Even today, there are still problems, even war.

When the promised child came, this produced two nations. These two nations are at war today, one against another. Both Abram and his wife did not patiently and faithfully wait. A lack of patience is also sin. A lack of faith has been known to produce sin. Lack of faith is not being There. I, too, am not There, if I do not have the faith to wait patiently on God's promises. From me, God desires dependence, patience and faith. If I allow fear and skepticism to control my spirit and mind, I am doubting God; therefore, I am not where I need to be in Him. I need to fall on my face at the foot of His mercy, in deep repentance, asking for overcoming faith. Even though there are trials, tribulations and obstacles, God remains faithful, never changing. His promises are current. Knowing how God keeps His word should produce strength among His creations, causing lives of faithfulness. Lives of faith affect others, and will future generations. I am depending on God to insert into my faithful prayers elasticity, with enough stretch to reach farther than near, reaching each future generation. Within Him, it is possible. I do not possess great wisdom or riches, as in materialistic things; but I have opportunity through God to be endowed with faith, and be faithful – faith to encourage and help others.

*In Judges 3:26-30 we find that Ehud's courageous zeal brought peace to Israel for eighty years.*

Genuine faith is a penetrator, even in perilous times; and will strengthen others spiritually, mentally and physically, giving them faith.

God's view is on faith, not age or position. He may work through unexpected conduits. I need to stay prepared for God to work through me, even for the blessings of others as well. I need to remain faithful. Solomon had great wisdom, but did not remain faithful to God. If I do not remain faithful to God, I am not There.

A non-persistent dependence on God is not evidence of genuine faith, and does not demonstrate, nightly or daily, a life of trust in God. When only a touch of faith is felt, if desired, God will turn it into flaming faith. Committed to Him, the flame will remain alive.

When enemies assail, when strength fails or earthly gains are lost, keep the faith. Job lost everything, still he did not lose faith in God. No matter what befalls, God does not change; therefore, let not the quality of faith change. Maybe, that just before a change of faith took place, God was about to perform a miracle or miracles. But, it can't be performed because of a lack of faith and patience.

God is the same today as in yesteryears. His word, His law, His love and will to help – no faith or wavering faith will hinder Him towards our needs. In God, there is tenderness, for His offspring (us). So many attributes God has, which are not seen with the naked eye, we need to look through the eyes of faith to see and obtain them. Sometimes, there is a faithless problem with the mind's and spirit's eyes' focus – there is not a problem with God's promises or power. His

Power is always there for us, and He has what is required to utilize it. I should be a faith utilizer of all; therefore, others will be strengthened in the faith, if they see or hear me tell of what great things I received from the Lord through faith. I need to share my faith. If I don't, I am not a conduit that God's miracles are able to flow through; I am a self-clogged channel. Therefore, I am not There.

By faith, I should walk and talk constantly beseeching the Lord to keep this mind which He created with unwavering faith of His will. God's will has not and will never change. It is recognized in His spoken word. For now, and forever, He wills that we are in His will, believing in Him, thus denying self. Even when joy is not felt, our faith should remain active. If it doesn't, we are not There.

If my being is only motivated by temporal things, things seen, producing emotional, happy, fleshly feelings, I am operating by non-spiritual feelings. Not by faith, but by sight and carnal feelings. Genuine faith clings, even when the death angel appears to claim. Can I say, if He should desert me, which He won't; yet, will I faithfully believe in Him? In works and deeds, I ought to faithfully perform for the Lord. He is my alternative. He is my joy, giver of joy. The Lord is an unsurpassed blessing, stabilizing faith and peace, the backbone of my strength for operating in the things of the Lord. Even when ambivalent feelings try to take residence, I must not deter. I must embrace endurance, letting the world see that my faith is real – real in what the Lord has done, is doing, and for the future – knowing that He is the God of the good times, and God in times of calamity.

***II Thessalonians 1:4:*** *So that we ourselves glory in you, in the church of God, for your patience and faith in all your persecutions and tribulations that you endure, the survival, strength, are in faith and patience in the strength of God.*

I must produce what it takes to activate God's strength, which is faith. I have no excuse; and, if I have, I am not There. Paul, in prison, did not curtail his ministry; he had grounds for excuses, still he persevered. He encouraged Timothy to be faithful. He said to him:

***II Timothy 1:5:*** *When I call to remembrance the unfeigned faith that is in thee, which first dwelt in thy grandmother Lois and thou mother Eunice, I am persuaded that in the also.*

The demonstration of these two women's faith greatly affected and influenced both Paul and Timothy. It is rewarding to be faith models in the world. As Paul encouraged Timothy, his spiritual son, so should we encourage God's offspring with the attitude of a pro, whoever practices with the ball. I need to constantly build my faith, remembering when I first believed. Faith is more than belief in certain deeds; it must materialize into growth of Christian character, self-control through God, who gives power, enabling me to be so. Yes, my faithful father.

***Ephesians 4:6:*** *One God and father of all who is above all, and through all, and in you all.*

I once had an earthly father, whom I had faith in. How much more I should have faith in my Heavenly Father Jesus, who, when I was a child, I learned of Him – about His awesomeness; who is able in all things and ways; who is presently with me, is able to be with me when I am leaving here, in a way that no one is able to. Also, after I will have crossed over. If I do not have faith in Him, I am so far from being There. I must have faith, which produces all of the necessities it takes for the manifesting of the faith needed to move Him into answering requests of His will. This, I pray for. Abraham had faith in looking for a city whose builder and maker is God, my father today and forever – invisible to the carnal sight, but was visible and seen by faith in the spiritual sight. That is the faith I am noising about. Wow, if I do not noise about Him, I am not There.

**Romans 4:20:** *He staggered, not at the promise of God through unbelief,*
*but was strong in the faith giving glory toGod.*

Along with faith, I must give Him glory for all, because it is all in Him. In accord to His will, I must be faithful.

**Romans 10:17:** *Faith cometh by hearing.*

Therefore, I must strive to shake off rebelliousness, and be attentive to the word of God.

**Romans 14:23:** *Whatsoever is not of faith is sin.*

Let us shake off doubts and fears, which are contrary to faith; the weight of it is sin. I want God to sanctify me with the faith that he has blessed me with. If I am established in the faith of Him, I am delivered from sin caused by lack of faith. In faith, ask God for things not of this world, things we do not see, or things that are not, which can only come through faith, the drawer manifested by God's power. From His realm, as He works through me by His commission, I shall harmoniously bring faith sheaves, being led by the comforter, the Holy Ghost, in comfort — directed by Jesus, the author and finisher of faith; also, the one who cares, and takes care.

**Matthew 6:30:** *Jesus said: Wherefore if God so clothe the grass of the fields, which today is, and tomorrow is cast in the oven, shall he not much more clothe you, oh ye of little faith?*

Jesus meant that, if God takes care of temporal things, how much more would He take care of us, his offspring, who are not as temporal as grass — whom he made possible everlasting life?

It is critical that we keep our faith currently strong and active. Fasting and praying for this are two among the main ingredients.

**Matthew 17:19:** *When the disciples asked of Jesus why they were not able to cast the devil out of the lunatic [Jesus had to*

*cure the lunatic], He said unto them, Because of your unbelief;*
*if ye have faith as a grain of mustard seed,*
*nothing shall be impossible unto you.*

Faith is based on the facts in God's word – and adherence to it.

Being faithful to walk in truth takes commitment; being faithful in avoiding errors, contrary to God's faith laws. I should walk faithfully in the narrow alley of holiness, by sight, and both in flesh and spirit, being well harnessed by faith.

If we do not, we are not There.

In God's zeal, oftentimes tests and challenges are imposed to strengthen our faith. If we become stagnant in our faith, creating a distance between God and ourselves, we know to pray to Him for restoration and to rekindle our faith. Also, we can apply God's word, which quickens and makes us alive.

As a youth, upon hearing about Jesus from Mom, also the preacher, I believed, and obtained and maintained burning faith in that man Jesus! I believe each thing I heard or read about Him. Faith that stood against ungodly walks, talks and habits, in and out of Daddy and Mom's presence – faith that shone, talked and taught in my parents' home. For all, I gave God the honor.

A faith with an effectual light that shone near and farther, causing others to embrace faith – a faith which emboldened me to kill poisonous snakes found on the property where we lived and toiled; even in the forest when we hunted for moss to supplement monies earned from crops – only, because God protected.

Faith enough to walk in waters of sloughs, ponds or gullies with my bare hands searching for turtles, which especially Mom loved to receive. Without God, I wouldn't have been faithfully emboldened. But, oh, my sisters and brethren, I gave God the glory – for the faith, bravery, protection, and guidance; His coat of arms, His hedge of thorns. If He hadn't endowed me with faith and bravery, I wouldn't have been so vivacious. Because of His protective watch, my cells were not penetrated by reptilian, poisonous fangs. In this body that God made, if need be, I want the fiery faith of youth to be restored and rekindled.

Though God doesn't exempt from seasonal suffering, still it is my intrinsic desire to lean on Him, forever being faithful to His calls; producing crops of goodly deeds. If I do not produce so that others can see and be strengthened, as a Christian, I am of very little value. I joy in what Jesus has done for me and others, and am confident for what He will do. My highest intellectual taste is for His will, in this life of His, called my life; after all, all of this being, called me, He owns and saves by His grace. This is the body that He has made.

**Ephesians 2:8:** *For by grace are ye saved through faith and that not of yourself.*

It is the gift of God, knowing this; I have loved more abundantly for Him.

If I do not have love for my Lord, I am not There.

I need to teach young people, not only teach, but live a life that teaches also, as Paul the Apostle did before Timothy and everyone. He said, in

> ***I Timothy 4:12:*** *Let no man despise thy youth,*
> *but be thou an example of the believers, in word,*
> *in conversation, in charity, in spirit, in faith, in purity.*

What a pitiful shame so many are living sin's deep impurities.

I need to hold to the faith, praying in faith for youth, that they repent, turn to God, grow to love Him, have faith in Him; with a determination to not want to lead them to lose faith, stumble, fall and remain in a fallen state. I want my life to remain an influential umbrella over their lives.

To the young sons and daughters, I exhort you to live a life which is pleasing to God. Those of you who aren't living in God's will, do not tarry – turn around, now.

The Bible says to remember the Lord thy God in the days of thy youth. Lives are more filling and useful if an early beginning was made in His vineyard. Though you may be talked or laughed about because of your faith, rejoice – knowing that it is for Jesus' sake. How He counted you to go through this for His sake, remembering how He, on the cross, paid a debt with suffering, and shed His blood for you. The apostles were beaten because they spoke in the name of Jesus.

***The Acts 5:41:*** *And they departed from the presence of the council rejoicing that they were counted worthy to suffer shame for His name; and daily in the temple and in every house, they ceased not to preach Jesus Christ.*

If I do not rejoice because I suffer for His name, I am not There. It is better to suffer for Jesus, rather than suffer because of sin. Faith exalts what God does for us. All are weak in some areas; but, God is our strength, if we faithfully lean on Him. God helps us when we are being attacked because of our faith. His Holy Ghost gives power for boldness in the things of our Lord.

***Romans 5:2-5:*** *By whom we also have access by faith in His grace, wherein we stand and rejoice in hope of the glory of God, and hope maketh us not ashamed – because the love of God is shed abroad in our hearts by the Holy Ghost, which is given unto us. We walk by faith, not by sight.*

When I am sprinkled with secular discomforts, through it all, I need to shake it off with joy and keep on working in His vineyard. If I am unable to endure, well, I am not where I need to be in the Lord. Surely, I am not There.

Again, I advise you youths to be faithful in the Lord. You are not too young. Josiah began to reign at the age of eight years old. Get in the run, where souls are saved – God's saving race.

Joseph's faithfulness helped his whole family. We may not see the results of our faith, but surely God honors faithfulness.

Sincere faith and prayers bring changes. Because of Hezekiah's faith and prayer, God healed him and saved the city.

*Hebrews 11:2:* By faith, the elders obtained a good report.

*Hebrews 11:3:* Through faith we understand that the worlds were framed by the word of God.

*Hebrews 11:4:* By faith, Abel offered unto God a more excellent sacrifice than Cain.

*Hebrews 11:5:* By faith, Enoch was translated that he should not see death.

*Hebrews 11:6:* But without faith, it is impossible to please God, for he that cometh to God must believe that He is.

*Hebrews 11:7:* By faith, Noah, being warned by God of things not seen as yet, prepared an ark to saving of his house.

*Hebrews 11:8:* By faith, Abraham, when he was called to go out into a place which he should after receive for an inheritance, obeyed; and he went out, not knowing wither he went.

*Hebrews 11:9:* By faith, he sojourned to the land of promise.

*Hebrews 11:10:* For he looked for a city which had foundations, whose builders and maker is God.

**Hebrews 11:11:** *Through faith, also Sara herself received strength to conceive seed, and was delivered of a child, when she was past age.*

**Hebrews 11:13:** *These all died in faith.*

**Hebrews 11:16:** *But now they desire a better country that is an heavenly, where God is not ashamed to be called their God.*

**Hebrews 11:17:** *By faith, Abraham, when he was tried, offered up Isaac; and he that had received the promise offered his only begotten son.*

**Hebrews 11:19:** *Accounting that God was able to raise him up, even from the dead.*

**Hebrews 11:20:** *By faith, Isaac blessed Jacob and Esau, concerning things to come.*

**Hebrews 11:21:** *By faith, Jacob, when he was dying, blessed both sons of Joseph, and worshipped, leaning on the top of his staff.*

**Hebrews 11:22:** *By faith, Joseph, when he was dying, made mention of the departing of the children of Israel, and gave commandment concerning his bones.*

**Hebrews 11:23:** *By faith, Moses, when he was born, was hid three months by his parents; they were not afraid of the king's commandment.*

> **Hebrews 11:24:** *By faith, Moses, when was come to years, refused to be called the son of Pharaoh's daughter.*

> **Hebrews 11:30:** *By faith, the walls of Jericho fell down after they were encompassed, about seven days.*

There are many more faith stories about the yesteryears of Biblical heroes.

Through faith, kingdoms were subdued, righteousness wrought, promises obtained, mouths of lions stopped. My faith needs to be genuine enough to stop lions' mouths, to stop the mouths of forked, wagging tongues, so that the evil spirits of such be as chaff before the wind, blown into the pit of fire.

By faith, weaknesses were made strong, violence was quenched, edges of swords were escaped; women received their dead, raised to life again; the blind received sight, the dumb talked; the lamb walked, the deaf ears were opened. Many were healed from diseases, demons, and transgressions.

Though Joseph had been sold to Pharaoh's men by his jealous brothers, because he was faithful and obedient to God, he forgave them. God blessed him; therefore, he obtained favor with Pharaoh, who granted him a high position in his realm. Joseph could have built a great empire for his own glory. He knew of the promised land, promised to Abraham. When famine invaded the land of his father back home, with a faithful, forgiving heart, he had his father and brothers transferred to where he abided in the land of plenty. Regardless of past suffering imposed upon him by his brothers, his faith in God remained alive. What a forgiving spirit.

If I do not, in obedience, and faithfully forgive, dying to self as Joseph, I am not There.

*Daniel 3:16: The three Hebrew children, Shadrach, Mesach and Abednego, refused to serve and worship the golden image of King Nebuchadnezzar, because they wanted to remain faithful to God Almighty.*

Faith in God makes troubling encounters fearless, or less fearful. Even if God wouldn't deliver them, still they determined to stay faithful. Also, they knew that God's eternal reward is worth more than any hurt they might endure.

God's word concerning faith is as current as when He first initiated faith. Therefore, let us embrace faith. If I do not embrace faith and exercise it with a glow visible to all, I am not There.

# Meekness

Another fruit of the spirit is meekness, which God looks for in order to be There.

Webster defines meekness as: gentle, patient, and mild.

Being born again, portraying all of the evidence of being born again in humility – that is how our Lord expects us to be. That is the nature He expects us to possess and demonstrate. Oh, to be in His will! Usually, the world makes a mockery of the meek followers of Jesus, labeling them as weak, spineless, naïve or cowardly, passive or pushovers. God doesn't want His meek followers to be trampled on or taken advantage of in a way displeasing to Him. But, He does want them to be enriched with wisdom, to demonstrate and utilize meekness as an effective light amongst the Christians and non-Christians. We must tour with qualities which God said we need to possess; to not have them means that God's will is not being obeyed. Jesus Himself is a meek and humble lamb. If we are lacking in these, we are not There.

Though, because of our transgressions, He is made to grieve or angered; therefore, chastisement is necessary. Which are the transgressor's fruits?  Which do not portray the spirit of meek seekers of God?

*Zephaniah 2:3: Seek ye the Lord, all ye meek of the earth, which wrought His judgment; seek righteousness. It may be ye shall be hid in the day of the Lord's anger.*

God values meekness; the meekness of God produces the humble weakness, a God requirement, for prayers to be answered.  When we are clothed in this weakness, then we are strong; that is when God is moved to our rescue.  Much is gained through meekness – by it, evil is rooted up and driven by non-violence power.  By it, reproaches are prevented; and pride is put to shame and slain, and humility is conceived and brought forth to live.

Where there is no meekness, there is shameless strife.

*Psalms 22:26: The meek shall eat and be satisfied; they shall praise the Lord that seek Him; your heart shall live forever.*

If we are not clothed with the above, and more, we are not There.

If I am meek, I shall be satisfied when I eat.  I shall praise the Lord.  Meekness promotes peaceful satisfaction and praises to the Lord.

*Psalms 25:9:* *The meek shall He guide in judgment;*
*and then will He teach His way.*

Constantly, I am asking the Lord to guide and teach me
His ways. Therefore, I must possess meekness, so that my
prayers are eligible to be heard and answered. Meekness, so
that I submit to His lead and guide – into abundant peace.

*Psalms 37:11:* *But the meek shall inherit the earth and*
*delight themselves in the abundance of peace.*

There is no peace as His peace. There is joy in His peace,
praise the Lord! There is beauty in the peace of the Lord.

Meekness increases joy in all who are meek.

*Isaiah 29:19:* *Meekness increases, also shall increase,*
*their joy in the Lord; and the poor among men*
*shall rejoice among the Holy One of Israel.*

Being a meek and humble lamb, as Jesus, affects everyone. Oh, to be as He!

I have that desire, but I have more growth, traveling, to
do. There is a place I have yet to reach. Oh, yes, that place
located in His perfect will. While journeying, I am sometimes accompanied by a broken, bleeding heart; but, I must
keep on keeping on, as Jesus, who bore a heavier cross. The
faith joy inside of me magnifies to aid my empathy; therefore, in strength of the Lord, I am able to travel on while

reaching. Jesus keeps on blessing, and I keep on thanking and praising Him.

If I stop, I won't make it to – There.

A meek person may be classified or viewed as a peculiar, distinctive being – naïve; or one who can't see farther than the nose's end. Peculiar people are likely to be single-eyed – not naïve, but submissive, dying to self, as the Bible says we who claim to be followers of Jesus should. In other words, as Jesus – humble as a lamb (a sheep), who never fight back, but weep and/or mourn.

**Titus 2:14:** *Whoso gave Himself for us [Jesus] that he might redeem us from all iniquity, and purify unto Himself a peculiar people zealous of good works.*

A meek-spirited person prefers to be on the giving end, rather than the receiving; is peaceable, gentle, easy to approach; feels that it is best to give, rather than receive, justice; feels that, by loving, fasting and praying for others who misuse us, could change them, thus moving them to God's plan. God loves all, despite what we are.

With an illumination, my meekness needs to glow. Wherever I am, being a non-respecter of person – Child of God – letting all know that they are loved.

**Proverbs 16:19:** *Better is it to be of a humble spirit with the lowly than to divide the spoils with the proud.*

We know that Moses was mightily used by God. Moses possessed a meek spirit. Because of his meekness, he was able to intercede for the grumbling children of Israel.

***Numbers 12:3:*** *Now the man Moses was very meek above all men which were on the face of the earth.*

***I Peter 3:4:*** *Even the ornament of a meek and quiet spirit, which is in the sight of God, is of great price.*

God values meekness, a quiet spirit, not boisterous; not rendering evil for evil, railings for railings, or loud exaltations of one's self. But, rather, loud in praising and glorifying God.

If I am not meek, the Lord will not give His word to me. I must be humble to receive His word.

If I am not, surely I am not There.

***Isaiah 61:1:*** *The spirit of the Lord God is upon me.*

Because the Lord had anointed me to preach good tidings unto the meek, He hath sent me to bind up the brokenhearted, to proclaim liberty to the captives, and the opening of prison doors for them that are bound. It is easy to preach to the meek. The meek, God is able to work with, and the meek will receive; therefore their brokeness will be healed. Those that are in bondage, God shall free. One has to be meek and humble, not stiff-necked.

Meekness brings God's blessings, spiritually, mentally and physically, even earthly gain of God's attributes.

>*Matthew 5:5: Blessed are the meek,*
>*for they shall inherit the earth.*

Meekness leads to and also brings God's blessings – spiritually, mentally and physically.  Other blessings provided by God, for the pleasure of his offspring – God has many rewards, which we do not always obtain, because His laws for obtaining them are sometimes not kept.

>*I Peter 3:4: But let it be the hidden man of the heart in that which is not corruptible, even the ornament of a meek and quiet spirit, which is in the sight of God's great price.*

God is a rewarder of the meek – no matter how man defines meekness of the Lord's will.

If I do not possess meekness that God honors, I am not There.

I must be able to die to self, though mistreated.  I must step back, and let the Lord of Lords intervene.

It is a delightful, fulfilling feeling, wholesome enough to fortify God's creation.

>*Psalms 76:8-9: The earth feared and was still,*
>*when God arose to judgment to save all the meek of the earth.*

My brothers and sisters, no matter how the world mocks you for being meek, I aspire that you embrace meekness. Let it be in you continually. The Lord is the rightful judge. He has the reward. Lean on Him. He is a solid prop.

**Psalms 147:6:** *The Lord lifteth up the meek;*
*He casteth the wicked down to the ground.*

This tells that the ones who are mockers of the meek are wicked ones. But, still, we must pray that they also repent, put on the armor of God, and embrace meekness. Let love abound. Hold on God is the rightful judge. As He is a meek and humble lamb, so should we be. If we are not, well, we are not There.

I have a strong desirous thirst for a completion in being There.

# Temperance

Temperance, another fruit of the spirit, which is also needed to be in God's commanded There.

Webster defines temperance as being temperate, moderate; or self-restraint, which is self-control.

If we do not possess these, we aren't There.

**Philippians 4:5:** *Let your moderation be known to all men. The Lord is at hand.*

God wants His offspring to operate in and with moderation, to be temperate even in dress, eating and drinking; to be abstemious, especially from transgression – which is sin – against God's will. Anything contrary to God's will is sin.

**II Peter 1:6:** *And to knowledge temperance, and to temperance, patience; and to patience, Godliness.*

Brothers and sisters, we need the whole armor. Know that all fruits of the spirit are needed, interacting as God intended. All are needed to make one eligible to be There, God's place.

Another definition of temperance is modification of attitude, not given to violence, a non-violent temper; operating in peace, caressed by agape love.

I need to operate in peace. I need to practice self-restraint, moderation in speech, attitude; even my countenance should be spiritually characterized by restraints. Restraints, as initiated by God – not causing small incidents to increase in magnitude; causing a widespread of confusion, hurt and bitterness, which could lead to hindrance to accepting God's plan among the brothers and sisters.

I need to walk, talk and look in a fashion that moderation is openly demonstrated; thus, drawing men, women, boys and girls to the knowledge of God's law. A lack of temperance, among those that are called by God's name, is known to create hindrances to His saving word. If I do not obtain and continuously practice temperance, I am not There.

I must abstain from sinful pleasures, willing to be kept; allowing God to keep me by His power. He is my strength and provider. He provides strength to all who, with a willing mind, as in faith.

**Philippians 4:7:** *And the peace of God which passeth all understanding shall keep your hearts.*

If I am willing, God shall keep me in His hold, as He faithfully did in the past, and still does.

**Philippians 4:13:** *I can do all things through Christ which strengeneth me.*

The strength which sustaineth this body called mine, which He created, which He owns, is strengthened by Him. When this body leans, He strengthens, propping upright.

**Psalms 94:18:** *When I said my foot slippeth, thy mercy, oh Lord, held me up.*

I know that my Lord is robed in strength. I want to possess knowledge in spiritual understanding in how to operate in moderation of self-discipline, preventing violent commotion. I desire a lifelong, non-violent temper, being able to approach others in meekness.

**Timothy 2:25:** *In meekness, instructing those that oppose themselves.*

Some teach that temperance (self-control) is not necessary, and that works don't save. No works alone don't save, but is one among other requirements. The Bible says that faith without works is dead. We need to operate in faith with action. If we do, surely God will make the necessary steps, causing us to grow to be as He. He wants to reproduce

His character in us, so that we can activate His love and other attributes. Praise God!

If I obey, letting Him guide me by His spirit, I shall develop self-control (temperance); not only in intake, but also in output. If I do not allow Him to, well, I am not There.

If I am taken by complacency, I want Him to ignite with His armor. I must fight boredom, impatience, with a determined will, commingled with prayer and fasting – with a continuous spirit of temperance. I must never tire from hearing the sound doctrine message, though I heard it over and over.

I need to bask in it. To do so is strength. For me, it is the basics. Remembering how I first came to believe, looking back, but going forward; knowing that, when I was reborn, God empowered me with His Holy Ghost, His goodness. I am a partaker of His divine, amicable nature. I must thrive to live in His will. I must persevere in fasting, praying and lifting Him up. All of this body that I am housed in, its organs, extremities, skin, bones, all five senses, spirit, mind and soul – all cells praise God Almighty! If I do not send praises for my maker, I am not There.

I must not only be a hearer of His word, but a reader and a doer, and divider of the revealed word of God. I must depend on Him for revelation, for wisdom, knowledge and understanding; also, discernment in recognizing those seeking to water the word down, who try to twist the truth to their comfort.

That I maintain the cloak of temperance, remembering that it is one of the ingredients God requires to line up with

His words, wherever I roam or abide, if I lack temperance, I am outside of God's will – and designated There. Oh, to be There is you, armored with the armor, to tear down strongholds.

The fruit temperance, if utilized by me through God's power, shall win battles presented by strongholds. If I have bowels of mercy and compassion, which are two of God's attributes, treating others with respect and courtesy, caring about and helping with their problems, then I am doing God's will. Still, in all, I need God's strength and guidance while being respective and humble.

Not a breather of tempestuous winds from my mouth, that chill others and promote storms of turbulence; that blow confusion to breed hate and bitterness. If I am a breather of such, I have lost the fruit of God (temperance). I am not There. Oh, Lord, allow the temperance of this soul to be as metal, fired in the furnace to gain glory and develop and stabilize the fruits of the spirit as a smith who makes and prepares metal objects with extreme heat of fire and beatings, fashioning them to his desired taste. Oh, Lord, do temper this temperance in this body, to Your eternal will, I pray.

Let me be stable and joyful, trusting in You, with temperance; because, if I am not stable and joyful, with furbished temperance, tempered by your fire, I am not There.

# Change – To Enter, There!

*Need to change your lifestyle; be adamant, practice innovations*

*Avoid using unnecessary words for expressions, be succinct*

*Let your thoughts, actions, and body language have right inclinations*

*Terminate exploiting habits, all confusion refuse to elicit*

*Shun ominous, avoid curt responses causing demoralization*

*Do not evoke dilemmas, do not malign, be truly altruistic*

*Develop a good rapport with others; be congenial, for good perceptions*

*Do not infringe inequity, operating in obscurity be explicit*

*Be a Godly role model; the only God some people will see is in our composition*

*Seek to reign with Him in longevity, this life is transient*


*VeLeJouSte*

# About The Author

## VeLeJouSte

Willie M. V. Stephens is the author of two previous books: *Rock In the Weary Land, and Exiting the Weary Land.*

Willie M. V. Stephens, avid worker for the Lord Jesus, is an inspiration to both young and old from all walks of life. Since childhood, she has been a firm believer in God, stressing the importance of serving the Lord, possessing good moral values, and obtaining education to be used to His glory. She emphasizes that, through God's power, with enduring faith, prayer, fasting and hard work, anything is possible.

She is often heard saying, "Get education to the glory of God, putting Him ahead. It is He who fashioned you with learning abilities; He is God! Reach for the skies." She is the mother of nine children (whom she dedicated to God while still in her womb), and her many talents include designer/seamstress, poet, gospel songwriter, etc. She often says, "I am a mother of nine, not one, two, three, or eight . . . but, nine. All are in my heart . . . what I want for one, I want for the others."

Growing up, Willie farmed with her Daddy and Mom. Afterwards, she married her husband, and they moved to a neighboring town. Willie has held numerous jobs with institutions and agencies such as the LSU Cooperative Extension – teaching nutrition while stretching dollars, Community Action, Juvenile Detention Center – working with the youth, several hospitals, and home health agencies. Willie has done volunteer work in the neighborhood, aiding LSU home demonstration agents in fashion. She also volunteered in the Community Center, teaching cutting and sewing. Willie became certified to work in nursing services as a C.N.A. She served as a church secretary, sang in the choir, and spoke in the church from text that she had written. Willie also is a witness of God to win souls. Additionally, she worked as an "extra" in playing a role in the movie "The Toy," in which Richard Pryor was the main actor.

She encourages that every day and every night we must walk with God, to build a bridge to that heavenly mansion not made with mortal hands. God does talk to her. He knows when the answers are needed. Through trying times, she would stress that we must "look for a brighter day." During illness, she would emphatically declare what is found in Isaiah 53:5: ". . . with His stripes we are healed." Willie feels that God can be trusted for anything. Even when our courage has been wrung dry, we should yet trust and worship God. She believes worship is a weapon and a burden destroyer.

Knowing that she has a charge to keep, a God to glorify, Willie continues to be an inspiration to her children and others. In all, she gives God the honor!

CPSIA information can be obtained
at www.ICGtesting.com
Printed in the USA
FFOW04n0313150317
33440FF